Creating a Music Website

Mike Simmons

PC Publishing

PC Publishing
Export House
130 Vale Road
Tonbridge
Kent TN9 1SP
UK

Tel 01732 770893
Fax 01732 770268
email info@pc-publishing.co.uk
web site http://www.pc-publishing.co.uk

First published 2001

ISBN 1 870775 72 4

British Library Cataloguing in Publication Data
A catalogue record for this book is available from the British Library

Printed in Great Britain by Bell and Bain, Glasgow

Contents

Dedication

I'd like to dedicate this book to two people, both of whom have been responsible for major changes in my life.

To a great friend, Paul White – without him I almost certainly wouldn't have come to write this book.

To Helen – who is, quite simply, the love of my life.

Introduction

The music industry is changing. Once upon a time the only way to make and sell records was to get a deal with a record company. Today, more and more musicians are going it alone. Building their own studios, recording their own albums and doing the marketing for themselves. The advantages are obvious – total creative freedom and a greater slice of the retail price finding its way back to the musician. There is one big disadvantage, however – without the power of the record company how is a musician going to reach the public?

Posters, sandwich boards, flyers and publicity stunts – they've all been tried and are well worth trying again. But what's new, and what makes it possible for a musician to reach the greatest possible market is the Internet.

A glance through any magazine or newspaper would lead the casual observer to believe that just about everybody has got their own email address, and that the majority of them have their own web site too. The fact that half of them don't bother to check their email, and that a good number of those web sites are either hugely boring or terminally self-indulgent is something of a disappointment, but nevertheless the Internet is having a considerable impact on our lives, and is now seen by many as a major source of information and entertainment.

The move by many Internet Service Providers to offer their customers free web space has led to a proliferation of new sites on the World Wide Web, and mine (musicfromthemountains.com) is one of them. I am a composer and musician, and the opportunity to advertise my music free of charge to the entire planet seemed pretty irresistible.

For the last four or five years I have been maintaining a site which tells people about my music and, equally importantly, sells it to them. I'm able to show them pictures of each of my albums, offer sample tracks for them to listen to and provide them with a range of useful links to other people's sites. Having a web site has also attracted people to my music who would otherwise never have heard of it – not least of these was a television company who used two of my tracks last year for a programme that they were making. If I hadn't had the web site their researchers wouldn't have found my music. If they hadn't have found the music they wouldn't have played it – and if they hadn't played it I wouldn't have had a nice cheque from the PRS!

Given that you've picked up this book the chances are that you're a musician too, and are wondering how the Internet could help you in your career. Over the next hundred or so pages that's exactly what we'll

This book started out in life as a series of articles in Sound on Sound magazine. These articles led to a surge of e-mails as readers posed question after question which I was happy to respond to. Clearly a book was called for, and here it is.

be looking at. I'll take you through the basics of setting up your own site, point out some of the pitfalls, and help you to produce a presence on the Internet that's worth visiting. We'll take it one step at a time and quite soon you'll be coding HTML with the best of them.

I need to assume that you're computer literate – that you know how to handle files and folders, for example, and are familiar with the workings of your word processor – but you certainly won't need to be a technological wizard.

Questions, questions, questions

What exactly Is the Internet?

The Internet consists of an indeterminate number of interconnected computers which are located throughout the world. Internet Service Providers (ISPs) such as Demon, AOL, CompuServe, and the like offer us access to that network, and once we have connected our computer to a modem, and a modem to the phone lines, our own computer also becomes part of the Internet, at least for the time that we maintain a telephone connection. We are then able to send and receive email, download files and, most importantly as far as this book is concerned, browse the World Wide Web.

From its beginnings the Internet has been a source of information, but gaining access to that information was initially a pretty unfriendly business, and for many the arcane knowledge required in order to download a file or join a newsgroup was a hugely inhibiting factor. With the development of the web, and the web browser, all this was to change.

What's a browser?

A browser is a piece of software which enables the user to view information on the web as 'electronic pages'. A web site is a collection of these pages, usually centred around a particular topic, which has been put together by one person or organisation. There will be links between the pages which allow the user to explore a subject with no more than the click of a mouse, even though the linked sites may be located as far apart as Neasden and Nova Scotia. As far as the user is concerned, a link is just a highlighted word or graphic which responds to a mouse click and automatically takes the user to another web site or a page within the same site.

All web sites, once constructed, reside on servers somewhere in the system (you don't actually need to know where); though some larger institutions such as universities and large companies may have their own servers, a private web site will generally end up on an Internet Service Provider's server.

A number of browsers are available, but the lion's share of the market is held by just two – Netscape Navigator and Microsoft's Internet Explorer, both of which are available for PCs and Apple computers. Both have undergone a number of upgrades and both are freely available from Internet Service Providers, freeware disks and by download from the Internet itself. If you haven't already got a copy of one or the other, and you want to produce your own web site, then you need to get one. If you want to do the job properly, you'll need both because, as we shall see, they don't always respond to the same information in exactly the same way.

Home page/web site – what's the difference?

These two terms tend to get used interchangeably, which can make it more than a little confusing for the newcomer since they are, in fact, different things. Generally speaking you can think of your home page as the first page that people see when they log on to (pay a visit to) your site. This single page might be the totality of your site but alternatively, it might be the gateway to several thousand other pages with a multitude of links between them. Both of these possible scenarios – the single page or the multitude of pages – are web sites, but however many pages your site will have, they'll all be accessed either directly or indirectly, from your home page. Every page on your site will, in fact, have its own unique Internet address think of it as a giant set of pigeonholes in hyperspace, each containing a single web page) but it's only the address of your home page that people need to know if they want to visit your site. Once in, they can work their way though your site to the other pages by means of those links. Think of your home page as your front door, and you won't go far wrong!

What is a URL?

An easy one! It's another name for an internet address. The letters stand for 'Universal Resource Locator'.

How does my web site get onto the ISPs server?

While you're creating your web site you'll be doing so on your own computer. You'll slowly build up a collection of pages, images, sound files and whatever, and they'll all be sitting on your hard drive. When you're ready to 'publish' your site – to let the world see it – then you beam the entire collection up to the ISP server, generally by means of a small piece of subsidiary software. Once the site is in place you can make any changes that occur to you simply by editing the page that still resides on your hard drive and then beaming that up to the ISP's server to replace the one that's already there. Adding pages is equally simple – create it on the hard drive, and send it to the server. It's probably easiest to think of that space on the ISP's server as another hard drive on your computer: what you put there is up to you, and you can change it just as often as you want.

I'm a Mac user – is that going to make any difference?

So am I, and no it's not. You've probably experienced all kinds of difficulties in the past, when PC users have handed you a floppy disk full of files, but you'll be glad to know that the HTML that a Mac reads is exactly the same as the HTML that a PC reads. There are certain differences in the way each platform interprets what it reads, but nothing that will cause you any major problems. Certainly when you're creating a site it makes no real difference which platform you're actually doing it on. I've designed sites using a Mac, I've designed sites using a PC, and I've even designed one site on both platforms simultaneously, moving from place to place with a bag fully of floppy disks. (On the whole, I think it's better not to ask!) It's really no problem.

What's HTML?

The information that a browser relies on in order to do its job is called HTML – Hypertext Markup Language. When a user clicks on a particular link within a web page, what they are really doing is sending a request for various pieces of data – text, pictures and so on – to be downloaded to their computer. Embedded in this data come HTML 'tags', the function of which is to tell the browser how the data should be arranged and displayed on the screen. HTML tags are easily recognised because they are always enclosed within angled brackets: instead of displaying them, the browser interprets them as instructions such as 'display the next paragraph in red', or 'make this picture a link to www.apple.com' or 'make this block of text a new paragraph' – and so on.

The example below shows an extremely dull web page, and the HTML code that went to make it.

Figure 1.1 A very dull page!

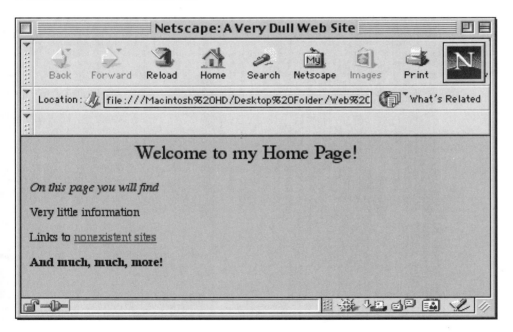

```
<HTML>
<HEAD>
<TITLE>A Very Dull Web Site</TITLE>
</HEAD>
<BODY>
<P ALIGN="center"><FONT size="5">Welcome to my Home Page!</FONT></P>
<P> <I>On this page you will find</I> </P>
<P>Very little information </P>
<P>Links to <A HREF="http://www.nosuchplace.com">nonexistent sites</A></P>
```

```
<P><B>And much, much, more! </B></P>
</BODY>
</HTML>
```

As I said, a very dull web page! It won't be long before you can do a good deal better yourself.

Hey, this all sounds a bit complicated – couldn't I get someone to do it for me?

Of course you can, if it all seems too daunting then you could always hire a professional to do it for you, but it's worth bearing in mind that some of the dullest web sites out there are the ones that someone has paid for. This is not to suggest that professional web designers don't know how to design web sites, because (most of them) do – rather, it's a reflection of the fact that time costs money, and people are often reluctant to pay for more than the minimum they need to get the job done. As a result they often wind up with very basic pages that anyone with a bit of time to spare could easily improve upon. Not only that, but unless you're going to pay someone to maintain the site for you (keep it up to date) then you're going to have to learn how do all this for yourself anyway – so why not start now?

Making a start 2

How do I set about creating a site?

Ah, I've convinced you! This is the really important question, the one that the rest of this book is dedicated to answering. Creating a web site is not half as difficult as it might seem. There are new skills to learn, of course, but if you know how to use a word processor (and there can't be many people reading this book who don't) then you're almost halfway there. Essentially, the process of creating your own web site breaks down into a number of stages:

> Designing the site
> Constructing the site
> Beaming it up to your ISP

Once your site is on your ISP's server, and thus available to the world at large (or, at least, that part of it with an Internet connection), there are two more stages to consider:

> Telling the world about your site
> Keeping it up to date

It's worth reminding you that there is no need to ever think of your site as 'finished' – particularly when you're doing it yourself. The more regularly you update the content of your site, the more likely you are to find that people tend to come back to it.

Designing the site

You need to consider what your site will look like, how many pages you're likely to need, what they will contain, and how they will be linked to each other and to other sites. If you're new to site design (and you probably are if you're reading this book), it's definitely worth spending an hour or two browsing the web looking at other people's sites to see how they're put together. See which elements work for you, and which don't. In particular, see how frustrating it can be to wait for some huge graphic to finish loading before you even know what a site is about. On the other hand, note how satisfying a well-thought-out site can be. It's not just the content of your site that matters – if you want people to keep coming back to your site you've also got to make it easy to use.

There are essentially two things to think about at the planning stage:

INFO

*J*ust as in any other piece of graphic design – this book, for example – there needs to be a balance between text, pictures and the all-important white space.

the look and feel of the site, and the way in which people are going to find their way around it. Graphic design is an entire subject in its own right, so if you're not confident in this area, either 'borrow' some ideas from other sites you like or enlist the help of someone with a good eye for composition. Inevitably your own taste is going to dictate how things look, because you'll want to produce a site that looks good to you, but you'd be very well advised not to go over the top too much with graphics and gimmicks. Keep in mind that huge blocks of text often go unread, and that while really big pictures might look pretty good once they've downloaded, there might not be that many people with enough patience to wait for that to happen.

Navigation

We've already discussed the relationship between a web site and a home page, but this is the moment to consider the way in which all the pages of your site are going to interrelate. As we've already seen, visitors to your site are going to find their way around by clicking on the various links that you put on your pages. There are a number of ways in which links can be organised; the choice is likely to depend on the size of your site and the material you wish to put on it. Unless you have a very small site, it's probably not practicable to put links to all your other pages on your home page.

Nor, at the other extreme, would you be likely to present the pages in a totally linear fashion where you can only proceed through the pages in a fixed order, see Figures 2.1 and 2.2.

Figure 2.1 (right) One page links to all
Figure 2.2 (below) One page links to another which links to another and so on

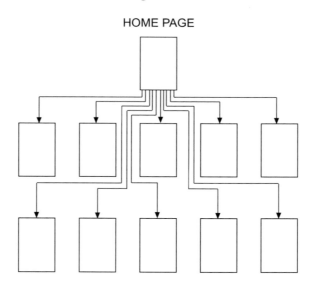

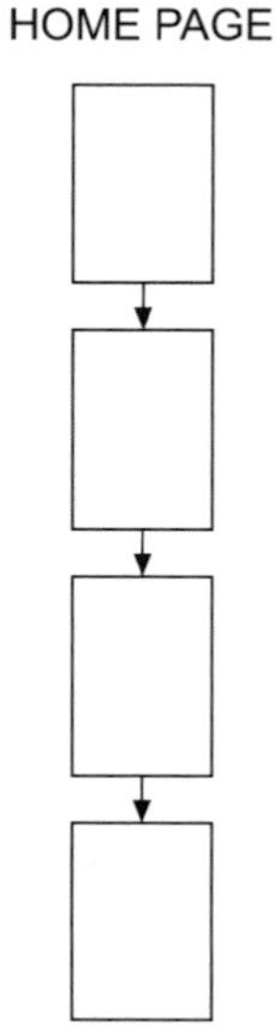

For most purposes a combination of the two approaches generally works best, but it's important that you should provide plenty of links directly back to your home page so the visitor doesn't get lost. Modern browsers always offer the opportunity to step backwards (to jump back to the previous pages you've visited) but you really should offer your visitor a more elegant solution than this.

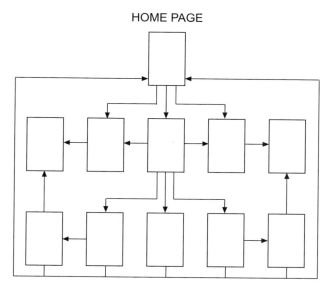

HOME PAGE

Figure 2.3 A happy medium!

Planning a web site is like painting a room – most of the hard work is in the preparation. So, get out that pencil – map out your site, get a sense of where the links are likely to be – and then you're ready to move into the construction stage.

Constructing the site

Having said that, we all know that in reality it's all that sanding down of surfaces that makes painting rooms so incredibly tedious, so If you really have managed to plan your entire site without jumping into the nitty gritty of coding then congratulations – it's more than I've ever managed! If you've just skipped over the planning stage entirely then make sure you don't go too far in your coding without getting out that pencil. You'll be sorry later if you don't – I usually am!

With that warning in mind let's get down to creating a site. You're probably wondering what software you're going to need and the good news is that it would be perfectly possible to create a web site with little more than this book and a word processor. In fact you don't even need a word processor, the text editor that seems to come with every computer operating system – Simple Text on a Mac or Notepad on a PC – will do just as well.

Authoring software

The process of writing some code, viewing it in a browser to see what it will look like, then writing some more code is a fairly straightforward but time-consuming business that requires little (little?) more than a cool head and a fair amount of concentration. The more complex your site is, however, the more difficult this process can become, and trying to identify a mistake that you've made in your coding can be something of a mind-numbing experience. It's this complexity of process that has led to the creation of a number of pieces of 'authoring' software, programmes specifically dedicated to web site creation.

> ### INFO
>
> *The text editor that seems to come with every computer operating system – Simple Text on a Mac or Notepad on a PC – will enable you to produce a perfectly acceptable web site.*

These range from the relatively simple Home Page or Page Mill, to the all-singing and all-dancing (and hugely coveted by this writer) Dreamweaver 4 which will facilitate just about every trick in the book. There are also a variety of shareware programs available, such as Web Weaver for the Mac or Home Site for the PC. Some modern word processors (such as Microsoft Word) will generate HTML code automatically (though this is sometimes somewhat unpredictable) and Netscape Navigator comes with a 'Composer' component which will also help you create web page. On top of that it will probably not have escaped your notice that a number of companies producing authoring software make 30-day limited versions of their programs available on the Web. You can get an awful lot of HTML coding done in 30 days...

Whatever software you choose, the common factor in all of these programs is that you assemble the page layout as you would like it to look (as you would in a DTP or word-processing program), and the software creates the appropriate HTML for you. For anyone who simply wants to set up a basic web site this is a pretty attractive prospect. No such software is foolproof, however. Things do go wrong and, when they do, an understanding of the code that's been generated can be invaluable. For this reason I shall assume in this book that you'll be doing the coding yourself, even if you're not – trust me, one day you'll be really grateful!

Page structure

Figure 2.4 The Web Page

OK, let's make a start. Have a look at the following web page, and the HTML that went to create it.

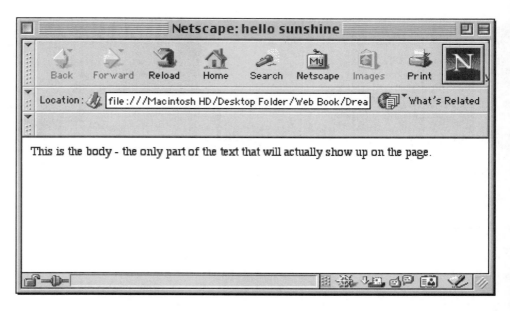

```
<HTML>
<HEAD>
<TITLE>hello sunshine</TITLE>
</HEAD>
<BODY>
This is the body – the only part of the text that will actually show up on the page.
</BODY>
</HTML>
```

Though it might not be apparent to the visitor to a site, every web page is made up of two discrete components – the Header, which is contained within <HEAD> tags, and the Body, which is, not surprisingly, contained within <BODY> tags. The entire page is contained with <HTML> tags – a declaration to the browser that it should treat the contents of the page as HTML.

The header section of a page can contain a variety of information about the page itself, but very little of the text that appears there will be displayed by a browser. The exception to this – and the only text there is in our example – is that any text written between the <TITLE> tags will appear on the title bar of the window displayed by the browser. It's not essential to provide a title for the page, but it generally looks rather more professional, and informative, than the 'Untitled' message that the browser will display if you don't! (By the way, don't make your title too long for the browser to hold. There's only a finite amount of space there and if your site visitor has resized their browser window your title may become truncated.)

Other data which may be stored in the HEAD section includes various 'META' tags which, amongst other things, provide information for search engines, thus making your site more likely to attract the attention of the casual inquirer. We'll come back to the META tags later. Let's get back to our example.

It's unlikely that you'll ever be confronted by anything quite as dull as the body section we've got here, but it still makes the point – for something to appear on your page, you must include it within the <BODY> tags. By the way, you'll notice that the second tag in every pair of tags contains a forward slash – this is standard practice, and tells the browser when a particular attribute should be switched off (so to say that something is 'within the BODY tags' means that it comes between the <BODY> and the </BODY> tags – and this is where most of the coding we'll be looking at in this book will be situated).

You might find it helpful to create this page for yourself. Switch on your computer, fire up your word processor, and type out the text exactly as I've written it. The important thing to remember is that you're going to need to save it as a text file. When you've finished entering the code go to "Save As" rather than "Save", and in the dialogue box that opens you'll see an option to save as "Text". Take that option, but save the file with the extender .html.

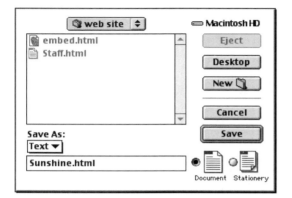

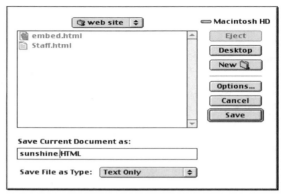

Figure 2.5 (left) Saving in
Claris Works, and
Figure 2.6 Saving in Word

Now let's see what it looks like on a browser on your computer. Depending upon how much memory you've got in your computer you may have to close down the word processor before opening the browser but if you can avoid doing this it'll make things a good deal easier for you as you start to create your own site. As your browser opens it may try to connect to the Internet – click on "stop" or "cancel" because on this occasion the page that you want to look at is not somewhere out there on the World Wide Web, it's on your hard drive.

It doesn't matter whether you're using Netscape Navigator or Internet Explorer at the moment but the process is a little different with each programme. If you're using Navigator then go to "File", "Open", "Page in Navigator" and select your saved text file. If you're using Internet Explorer then simply go to "File", "Open File" and, again, select your file.

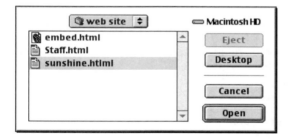

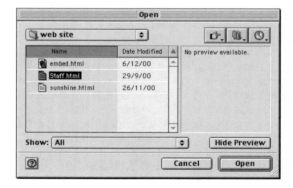

Figure 2.7 (left) Opening a
page in Netscape
Figure 2.8 ... and in Internet
Explorer

So, there's your first web page up and running in a browser. Not too exciting, is it? You'll be glad to know that you don't just have to use plain text. Try modifying the the text between the <BODY> tags as follows:

<B>This is the body – the only part of the text that will actually show up on the page.</B>

and open it again in your browser. Yes the <B> stands for bold! If it didn't look bold in your browser just try clicking the "reload" or "refresh" button and it will. So what was happening there? After you edited your text file your browser was still displaying the old file, and needed to be told to look at that file again before it could display the changes you've made. If the text still didn't look bold my guess is that you forgot to save as a Text File when you re-saved your document.

Now try this:

```
<I>This is the BODY – the only part of the text that will actually show up on the page.</I>
```

and you'll see that I stands for italic. You want bold and italic? No problem at all, just try this:

```
<B><I>This is the BODY – the only part of the text that will actually show up on the page.</I></B>
```

You'll see the tags are "nested", that they are switched off in the same order that they were switched on. It's important to make sure that you always follow this convention as some browsers can become confused if you don't. (and no-one wants a confused browser!) If you'd like to underline some text then you can probably guess what the <U> tag does – but don't forget that closing </U>!

It's also possible to make a selected part of your text flash on and off like the neon sign outside a particularly dodgy motel. I could tell you how to do it, it's incredibly easy – but I'm not going to do so. Flashing text is widely recognised as being seriously tacky and is a clear sign of someone with very little taste.

You will have noticed by now that however many times you hit the space bar when you're entering text in an HTML page, those spaces don't seem to appear when you open up the page in a browser. The same is true of carriage returns: your document may appear to be neatly laid out into paragraphs when you look at it in your text editor or word processor, but when you view it in a web browser it just seems to be one huge mass of text. This would seem to have pretty severe implications but, luckily, help is at hand.

Have a look at the following piece of coding:

> **TIP**
>
> *Whenever you're coding HTML by hand and find your browser isn't displaying your work as you expect it to, check you have "refreshed" the page and that you have saved your file "as text"*

> **TIP**
>
> *Don't use flashing text! Ever! Believe me, I'm looking after you here, don't do it!*

```
<BODY>
<P>first paragraph first paragraph first paragraph first paragraph first paragraph first paragraph first paragraph</P>
<P>second paragraph second paragraph second paragraph second paragraph second paragraph second paragraph second paragraph</P>
<P>here is a pair of lines<BR>without a paragraph break between them</P>
<P>        and here is some indented text</P>
</BODY>
```

and then see how this appears when it's opened in a browser

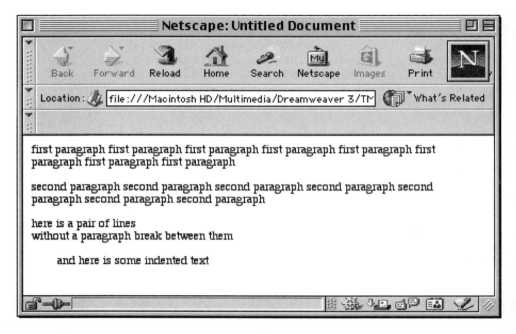

first paragraph first paragraph first paragraph first paragraph first paragraph first paragraph first paragraph first paragraph

second paragraph second paragraph second paragraph second paragraph second paragraph second paragraph second paragraph

here is a pair of lines
without a paragraph break between them

 and here is some indented text

Figure 2.9 The Web Page

So what's happening? The <P> and </P> tags identify each paragraph, and the <BR> tag (which doesn't need a closing </BR> tag) forces a new line without creating a paragraph. And that ' ?' Each one of those indents the line from the left by one space. An alternative to ' ' is the <BLOCKQUOTE> tag, which will indent a line, or an entire block of text, but needs a closing </BLOCKQUOTE> to end it. You can have several nested <BLOCKQUOTE> tags if you want to indent something even further, but you'll need an equal number of </BLOCKQUOTE> tags at the end of the text. Pretty nifty you may think, but there's more to come!

Colour

Let's think about adding a touch of colour to your page. Do you remember the extremely dull web site we looked at on page 3? Let's see if we can brighten it up a little. You may already have typed out the code but if not do it now. Yes that is dull! Now try replacing that first line with this:

```
<P> <FONT COLOR="#FF0000">Very little information </FONT>
</P>
```

Save it as a text file, and view it in your browser again. Now look what you've got – red text! At least, you'll have got red text if you remembered to use the American spelling of "colour" rather than the English. It's worth making this point now – if you make a mistake in your coding, particularly with your spelling, then you can't bank on getting any kind of error message; your code will simply be ignored by the browser. So, if you want coloured text it's got to be COLOR – COLOUR simply won't do.

Hex code

You may be wondering about that "#FF0000". It's what's called Hex Code and is one of the ways in which colour is described to a browser. There are other ways to do this but they're not so reliable, so for the time being let's stick with Hex.

Try this for the third line:

```
<P> <FONT color="#FF0000">much </FONT> <FONT color="#00FF00">much</FONT>
<FONT color="#FF00FF">more</FONT> </P>
```

...and you may wonder whether you're slipping back into the 1960s.

Those of you who remember your colour wheels from primary school may have spotted that each pair of two hex digits refers to the proportion of each of the primary colours (red, green and blue respectively) involved – so, for instance, yellow contains the full amounts of red and green, but no blue. The lower the values, the darker the colour – a value of 7F7F7F (hex FF is equal to decimal 255, and 7F to 127), for example, will display all three primaries at half strength, giving a mid grey.

By the way, I bet you weren't able to resist clicking on that "nonexistent sites" link in the third line. What did you get? A broken link message. Broken links are something to avoid at all costs, but on this occasion it was unavoidable because I made the link address up – I told you it was a nonexistent site! We'll be coming back to links in a little while, but meanwhile, back to our colours:

Background colour

Try replacing that first <BODY> tag with this:

```
<BODY BGCOLOR="#0000FF">
```

and you'll see that in the same way that you can control the colour of the text, you can also control the colour of the background.

By the careful manipulation of text and page colours it's quite possible to ensure that absolutely nobody will be able to read your site at all, or at least not without suffering from extreme nausea! Those of us old enough to remember Oz magazine may experience some small twinges of nostalgia here but, if the purpose of your site is to communicate, then it's worth considering whether the colours you choose help or hinder this process. As I've said before, it's a good idea to visit other people's sites and see what works and what doesn't.

Font size

Before we move on, have a look at this piece of HTML, and the web page it produces:

INFO

Any piece of text can be any colour you want it to be – you just need to know the correct hex code to enter between the <FONT color> tags. Here are a few more Hex codes for you to experiment with:

#000000 = Black
#FFFFFF = White
#FF0000 = Red
#FF00FF = Magenta
#0000FF = Blue
#00FFFF = Aqua
#FF00FF = Magenta
#00FF00 = Lime
#00FFFF = Cyan
#FFFF00 = Yellow

```
<HTML>
<HEAD>
<TITLE>Sizes</TITLE>
</HEAD>
<BODY>
<P><FONT SIZE="1">Hello</FONT> </P>
<P><FONT SIZE="2">Hello </FONT></P>
<P><FONT SIZE="3">Hello </FONT></P>
<P><FONT SIZE="4">Hello </FONT></P>
<P><FONT SIZE="5">Hello </FONT></P>
<P><FONT SIZE="6">Hello </FONT></P>
<P><FONT SIZE="7">Hello</FONT></P>
</BODY>
</HTML>
```

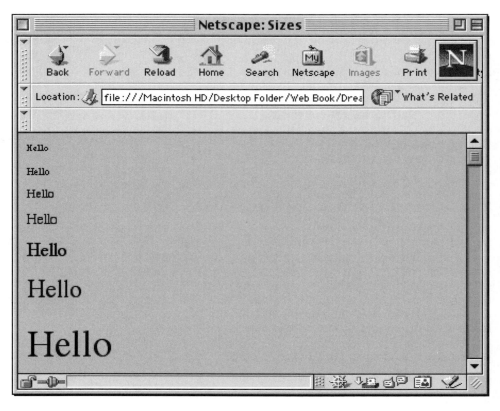

Figure 2.10 The Web Page

As, you can see, we're not restricted to just one FONT size – simply introduce the <FONT SIZE> tags into your coding and you've suddenly got much more control over the way in which words will appear on the screen. By the way, the default size for text is <FONT SIZE="3"> so you never really need to write that code – it's taken for granted unless you state something to the contrary.

Headings

Given that you can now produce text large enough to make a heading, you may be wondering how you can coax it into sitting in the centre of a line rather than sticking to the left margin. The answer is to add a component to the <P> paragraph tag:

```
<P ALIGN="center">Dull Text Page</P>
```

I'll leave you to work out what the align="right" and align="left" tags do! In each of these examples I've tended to demonstrate one tag at a time, but this is only for the sake of clarity. As we've already seen with our <B> and <I> tags, It's perfectly possible, and usual, to combine as many tags as you need to get the desired result – just make sure that you don't forget any of the closing tags while you're doing this, and that they're nested. Before we go any further, see if you can work out what this would look like before viewing it in your browser:

```
<P ALIGN="center"><B><FONT size="6" color="#FF0000">Dull Text Page
</FONT></B></P>
```

Yes, large red text, centred and emboldened. Did you get it right?

Just to confuse things a little, there is also a range of <H> tags, ranging from 1 (the largest) to 6 (the smallest) which are specifically designed for headings. The <H> tag doesn't simply determine the FONT size, it also works like the <P> tag, creating a break between the previous paragraph and the line on which your Header is displayed: you can also use components such as 'align' in the same way. It's something of an anomaly that the smallest <H6> is a great deal smaller than the largest standard FONT size, but you may find it a useful refinement.

Thus, the following would display a centred Header on a new line, in the largest size of text:

```
<H1 align="center">Dull Text Page</H1>
```

Fonts

You will have realised by now that regardless of what font you type your HTML in, when you open up your work in a browser it will always be the same. Let's take a small detour here and find out what's going on.

When you design a page for a magazine or book you can do so with a fair degree of confidence that what you design is what your reader will ultimately see. If you're designing a web page you can have no such confidence.

To find out why just try this – Boot up your favourite browser, go to 'Preferences' (then to 'Appearance' in the case of Navigator) and then go to 'Fonts'.

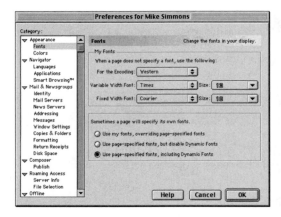 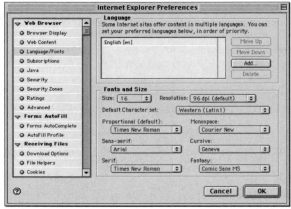

Figure 2.11 Netscape
Preferences and Internet
Explorer Preferences

You'll see that the appearance of any web page can be changed dramatically if the user simply chooses to select a different default font type or size in the browser preferences. In other words, the person with the browser decides what font your pages are going to be displayed in, rather than you!

Unless we introduce a further piece of HTML, that is. Try the following piece of code:

```
<FONT FACE="Arial"> Now I've got some control over what my text looks like!</FONT>
```

and open it up in your browser. It really does look as if you do have some control – but now try this:

```
<FONT FACE="nosuchfont"> Now I've got some control over what my text looks like!</FONT>
```

and see what happens – you're back to your default font again.

Unless you happen to have a font installed on your machine called "nosuchfont", that is, because what the <FONT FACE> tag is really doing is saying to your visitor's browser "This is the font I want this text displayed in if you've got it installed on your machine. Otherwise go with the default".

There's a much better chance of this working with a common font such as Arial but you can present the browser with a preferred range of fonts with something like

```
<FONT FACE"Arial, Helvetica, sans-serif">Now I've got some control over what my text looks like!</FONT>
```

The message going to the browser here would be "If you've got Arial installed use that, otherwise try Helvetica, otherwise try sans-serif and good grief if there's nothing else you better use the default."

What this means, of course, is that we do have some control over how our text appears, but we can never be sure that it appears the same way for everybody.

Lists

Sometimes we want to display information in a more structured fashion than is possible with simple paragraphs. Fortunately, the resources are available within HTML to do this. Have a look at the following code and see how it looks in a browser.

```
<HTML>
<HEAD><TITLE>LISTS</TITLE></HEAD>
<BODY>
<BLOCKQUOTE> <P><FONT size="5">Dear Father Christmas</FONT></P>
</BLOCKQUOTE> <P>Here is a list of things I would <B>really</B> like -</P>
<UL> <li>A new synth</LI>
<LI>A copy of Flash</LI>
<LI>A nice holiday</LI> </UL>
<P>This is the order in which I'd like to have them -</P>
<OL> <LI>A nice holiday</LI>
<LI>A copy of Flash</LI>
<LI>A new synth</LI> </OL> </BODY> </HTML>
```

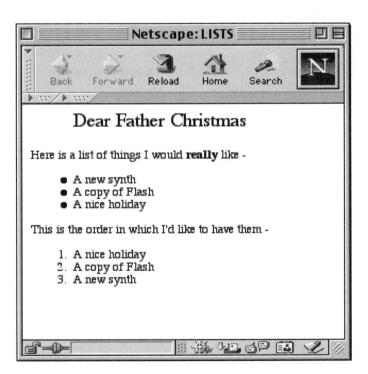

Figure 2.12 The Web Page

Some of the code will be fairly familiar by now, but some of it less so.

One thing you'll probably notice is that I've put all the <HEAD> and <TITLE> tags on the same line. The only reason for putting each tag on a separate line is that it makes it easier to read – as far as the browser is concerned, it makes no difference whether it's presented like that or as one dense block of text; carriage returns are ignored. As long as the tags are all in the right places it'll know what you want it to do.

So, on with the code. You'll see I've used <BLOCKQUOTE> for the heading, and made it a little larger with the <FONT SIZE="5"> tag. The next line is treated as a paragraph – in that it's on a line on its own – and I've used the <B> tag to embolden the word 'really'.

After this, you'll see the <UL> tag. What this does is tell the browser to expect an 'unordered list' – a series of individual text items which the browser will display on separate lines, each preceded by a bullet point. Following the <UL> declaration, each item in the list is held between <LI> and </LI> tags. The next list is almost exactly the same, except that it's an 'ordered' list, which is indicated by the <OL> tags. These work in exactly the same way, except that the browser automatically numbers each item rather than using bullet points. Would you like Roman Numerals instead of Arabic? No problem, just use <OL TYPE="I"> instead of <OL>. For a lettered list, you could try <OL TYPE="A">. You want different kinds of bullets? Replace the <UL> tag with <UL TYPE = "SQUARE"> or <UL TYPE="CIRCLE"> – it must be magic!

Figure 2.13 More lists

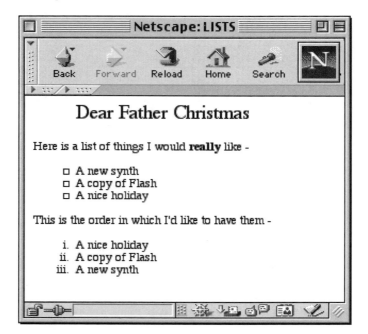

Bells and whistles

You may have seen bullets on other people's sites that were even more interesting – shiny spheres, flashing lights, dancing ducks, and the like. They certainly brighten up a site (as long as they're not overdone) and look a good deal more interesting than any of the lists that we've looked at so far.

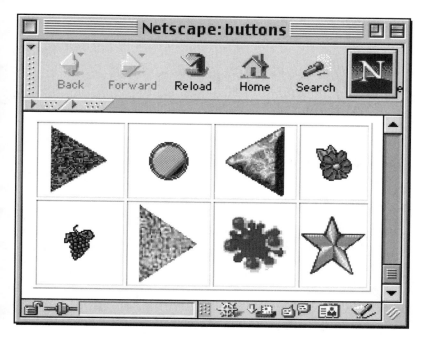

Figure 2.14 Shiny spheres and flashing lights certainly brighten up a site

If you'd like them on your site it's easily done – but you won't create them with HTML. You want to know how to do it? OK, let's start by talking about pictures.

3 Working with graphics

Pictures on the web

It would be quite possible to fill your entire web site with nothing but text if you wanted to, but it might not look very attractive if you did so, and you might find that your visitors didn't stay there for very long. One of the things that's made the web what it is today is the facility to add pictures, but working with images is not without it's implications. Whatever anybody else may tell you, when it comes to adding pictures to your web site, size really does matter. Graphics files are much bigger than text files and though they certainly brighten up a page, pictures also slow down the speed with which that page will load into the browser – and the larger the file size for each picture, the slower things will become.

It's always important to bear in mind that most people gain access to the internet via a modem, and that even the very fastest modem is not that fast at all. There are some lucky people, of course, who log on at work or college via much faster ISDN lines, and we're all holding our breath to see what ADSL might bring (Yes, this is the paragraph with lots of unfamiliar acronyms!) but it's going to be some time before anything other than a modem is the norm. It makes sense then, to make sure that your graphic files are as small as they possibly can be.

So far everything that we've done can be achieved with nothing more than a text editor or word processor, but when it comes to working with pictures, things are not quite so straightforward. Though the web itself is a rich resource of photographs and clip art which you are often able to use on your own site, the moment you want to start using your own pictures, you really need to start thinking about acquiring another piece of software – a graphics program. You'll need this because:

You might want to adjust the size of an image.
You might want to crop the image, or edit something out from it.
You might need to change the resolution of an image.
You might want to change the number of colours used to display an image.
You might want to convert between file formats.
You might want to create an image "from scratch" with drawing tools.

The leading software for image manipulation is undoubtedly Adobe's Photoshop, but this may be rather more than you need – or wish to budget for – when you just want to tinker with a few images for the web. Happily there a wide variety of shareware programs (Graphic Convertor for the Mac and Graphic Workshop for Windows spring to mind) which will meet pretty much any requirements you might have.

Alternatively, the software that comes with many scanners might well fit the bill. If you want to transfer a lot of pictures onto your web site from prints, drawings or other "hard-copy" media, then a scanner might well be a worthwhile investment. Though some photographic shops and print bureaus will scan material for you – at a cost – you simply don't have the same degree of control that's available when you do it yourself.

You don't need an elaborate scanner to get the kind of picture quality required for presentation on a web site, but if you're going to buy one to do other jobs, scanning material that is eventually to go to print, for example, then it's best to spend a little more on a model that can scan at a resolution of 600dpi (dots per inch) or better. If you're only interested in creating web pictures, then £100 or less may buy you a perfectly serviceable model, but for more serious use, expect to pay upwards of £150 – though it's still worth checking prices, since they seem to be falling all the time.

Whether you're producing illustrations with a graphics program or scanning in your own photographs, the most important thing to bear in mind is that you need to be sure that the quality is as good as it can be, but no better than it need be. As I've already hinted, most scanners are able to scan at a range of different resolutions – and there are many machines offering anything up to 2400dpi or more. The higher the resolution the greater the fidelity in the scanned image, but there's little point in producing a picture at 300dpi, for example, when most monitors are only capable of displaying a resolution of between 72 and 90dpi. Similarly, your picture may well look at its best when displayed in a format that stores millions of colours – but just how much worse would it look in a 256-colour palette, which would make for a far smaller file? And what about black and white, which would make it much smaller still? Your graphics program will let you experiment here, but always bear in mind that the smaller the final file is, the faster it will load into your site visitor's browser – and the sooner it does this, the less likely they are to lose interest and go to another site.

File formats

Two file formats, called GIF and JPEG, are the standards used for web graphics (and hence supported by most browsers), and choosing the right one to store your images is also important in keeping file sizes to a minimum, since each uses different compression systems optimised for different types of image. Most graphics programmes will allow you to save your image as either file type (just go to "Save As" in the file menu) but you'll find GIF is best for line art or anything else where there are fairly large blocks of a single colour, whereas JPEG is often a better format for more complex images such as photographs. If you're not sure which is best for a particular image, save the file as a GIF and see what

INFO

Graphic Convertor for the Mac and Graphic Workshop for Windows are good shareware programs that will help you edit images for your website

it looks like and how big the file is. Then compare it with the same image saved as a JPEG.

Once you've decided on your file type you may, depending on your graphics package, be able to reduce the size of your file even more. JPEGs can be saved at different levels of compression; but the greater the level of compression, the more degraded the image is likely to become. However, it can take a keen eye to notice on a computer screen what would be startlingly obvious on a printed page. Similarly, the size of GIFs can be minimised by reducing the number of colours in the palette used to reproduce them.

There's nothing wrong with a bit of trial and error here as long as you remember the one golden rule – if it looks good enough on a monitor then it probably is good enough.

It's worth mentioning that there are a number of pieces of software which are specially designed to optimise your images for the web, the inestimable Fireworks probably being the most popular. If you really want to reduce the size of your graphics files to an absolute minimum then this is the software for you, but it's not cheap and you may want to see how well you can do on your own before making such an investment. The only real price you'll pay for doing this is one that you'll pay in time. Just remember though, a picture may well be worth a thousand words, but however small you make it, it'll still take an awful lot longer to load!

TIP

Do all that tinkering on a copy of the graphics file rather than the original. Some of it is irreversible, so if you haven't got a copy to fall back on you may well be stuck!

Figure 3.1 The smaller the file the faster it will load – four variations when working with Fireworks

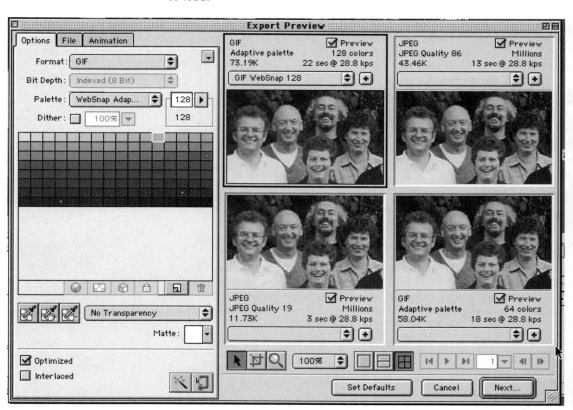

Adding pictures

So, how do you get a picture onto your web page? The following piece of HTML...

```
<IMG SRC="aber2.JPG">
```

located somewhere between the <BODY> tags will add a picture (in this case, one called aber2.JPG) to your page.

It's perhaps worth being a little more precise in our terminology here, because it won't really add the picture to the page at all, it will simply *appear* to do so. In order for someone else to see that page as you want them to, they'll need both the file with the HTML code that says <IMG SRC="aber2.JPG">, and the graphic file called aber2.JPG as well. They won't actually be aware of this, the browser will do all the fetching and carrying for them, but in order for this to work both files will need to be in the same relative position on the ISP's server as they were on your own hard drive, otherwise the picture will appear as nothing more than a broken link.

Recap

It's worth us taking a short detour here and recap what we know so far. When you've completed your site (or at least got it in a good enough state to publish it as a first edition) you'll beam it up to your ISP's server. Until then you'll be building the site on your own computer. The more work you do, the more files you'll accumulate – one for every page, one for every picture, one for every sound file, and so on.

If you're a methodical kind of person you'll immediately start by creating a series of folders for each type of file. Alternatively, you may have them strewn all over your desktop, intending to tidy them up later. The moment you do tidy them up you'll be in for a bit of a surprise, because every link you've made will have been broken!

Let's look at that <IMG SRC="aber2.JPG"> again. Besides anything else, it tells us that the image file is in the same folder/directory as the page file. Alternatively,

```
<IMG SRC="pictures/aber2.JPG">
```

would tell us that the image file is in a folder called 'pictures', which is in the same folder as the page file. Part of the HTML is a path, telling the browser where to find the picture. If you move that picture into another folder then it simply won't be able to find the file. However, provided you make sure the path to the file is always correct, it won't matter if you continue to edit the file, nor does it matter if you replace it with another file of the same name. What this means is that if you start off with a series of folders before you start constructing your site you're likely to avoid a lot of extra work later on.

Some authoring programs manage the whole site for you and won't let you make this kind of mistake. Others will, however – and I speak from experience! It's probably worth mentioning at this point that all

> **TIP**
>
> *If you start off with a series of folders before you start constructing your site you're likely to avoid a lot of extra work later on.*

your file names should consist of no more than eight letters (plus extender). For Mac users – and PC users whose operating systems have finally caught up with Macs – this can come as something as a shock, but not every ISP's server will recognise a file with a name like 'My Summer Holiday in France', however sensible that name might seem to you!

So, back to the pictures. Consider the following piece of HTML:

```
<IMG SRC="lleyn2.jpg" WIDTH="365" HEIGHT="244" ALT="cottage">
```

First you'll see that the file 'lleyn2.jpg' is called onto the page, in just the same way that we called up 'aber2.JPG' in our previous example, but now the size of the image is also specified. The advantage of doing this is that we tell the user's browser what to expect, and so help it to display the page rather more quickly than it would otherwise. The measurements are in pixels and, if you are using authoring software, the data is likely to be inserted automatically.

If you're coding by hand then you should be able to get the dimensions from your graphics package – look for a menu option something like "get info" and you should find the size in pixels displayed for you if it's not already on the screen. In point of fact we could make the image much smaller, or bigger, than its normal size simply by altering those figures but doing this is not without its implications, as we shall see a little later.

So what about that ALT "cottage"? It's worth bearing in mind that not every browser displays pictures, and that not every user of more modern browsers chooses to have that option switched on. The ALT text is what is displayed in place of the image while it is loading, or instead of the image if the browser has not been configured to show them. It is also what is read out by text-to-speech software on browsers used by the visually impaired. In addition, some browsers will display the ALT text as a 'tool tip' if the cursor is held over the displayed image.

One further piece of HTML: try inserting an image into a page and then typing in some ordinary text. View what you've done in a browser and you'll see the picture displayed first with the text beneath it. But what if you want the text beside the image? Insert an "ALIGN" command as follows:

```
<IMG SRC="lleyn2.jpg" WIDTH="365" HEIGHT="244" ALIGN="LEFT" ALT="cottage">
```

And now you'll see the text running all the way down beside the image (Figure 3.2).

I'll leave you to guess what happens if you try ALIGN="RIGHT"!

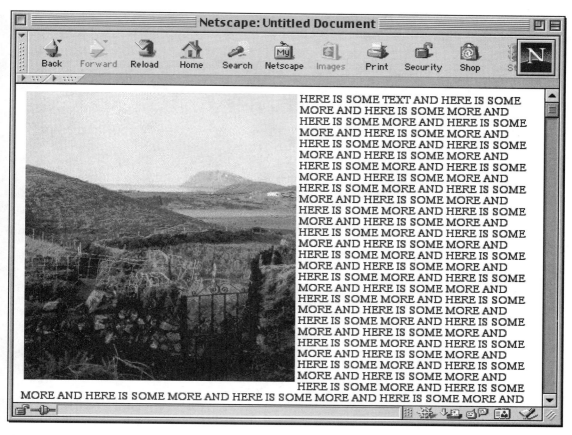

HERE IS SOME TEXT AND HERE IS SOME MORE AND

Figure 3.2 Wrapping text round a picture

Tiled backgrounds

One technique that can help to add a professional and individual look to a site is something called 'tiling'. This is a process whereby a small image, either in GIF or JPEG format, is repeated again and again throughout a page to act as a background to the text. You can do this very easily, simply by replacing the <BODY> tag in your HTML document with <BODY BACKGROUND="filename">.

It's worth reminding you again that this piece of code will only work if the tile file is in the same folder as the page actually using it. If the image was in a folder called "graphics", for example – which was in the same folder as the actual page – you'd need

```
<BODY BACKGROUND= "graphics/filename">
```

instead.

As always with generic web graphics, you have a choice between designing your own, or using ones that someone else has made. Vast quantities of ready-made files for background tiles, arrows, buttons, spacers and the like are widely available for free download on the Internet.

Here are just a few web addresses where you can find ready-made files optimised for the web:

www.best.com/~drzeus/Art/Textures/Textures.html
www.netscape.com/assist/net_sites/bg/backgrounds.html
http://netcreations.com/patternland/

Alternatively, it's an extraordinarily easy piece of work to do yourself – if you just follow a few basic rules.

- Firstly, remember that the browser will still have to download the file to display it so, as always with web graphics think in terms of small file sizes – perhaps optimised by using a small number of colours, small dimensions or a high degree of file compression. As a guide, a typical background tile might measure something like 125 pixels square, with the file weighing in at 1 or 2K.
- Secondly, make sure that your tiled background is subtle enough not to overpower the text that it's a background to and
- Thirdly, make absolutely sure that the GIF or JPEG extender is on that filename. I've forgotten to do this several times, and while my browser seems quite happy to display the file straight from the hard drive, it's a very different story once the site is up on the server! In case you were wondering – and I hope you were – the closing tag for <BODY BACKGROUND> is simply </BODY>, as it is for the normal <BODY> tag.

Text as pictures

As you already know, HTML is a mark-up language, and simply tells the user's browser how to set up a page. Consequently, however something may appear on our machine, it's impossible to dictate exactly how it will look on someone else's. When we were talking about text I explained how the <FONT FACE> tag could be used to tell a browser what font a particular piece of text should be displayed in, but these instructions will still only work if that font is installed on the end user's machine.

There is a way round all this which will always work, but it's really only viable for very small pieces of text. I'm very fond of a font called "Marker Fine Point" and wanted to use it for the heading on each of my pages. Given that it's a rather obscure Mac shareware font it's unlikely to be installed on many of my visitor's machines, so the only way that I could use it was to save the text as a picture (Figure 3.3).

This simply meant opening up a graphics programme and typing in each of my headings there. Cropping the image as closely as I could do and then saving it as a .GIF resulted in a file of only 3K and enabled me to call the title up with something like:

```
<IMG SRC="title.GIF" WIDTH=294 HEIGHT=51>
```

In this way I was able to ensure that it would always appear in the font of my choice rather than that of my visitors!

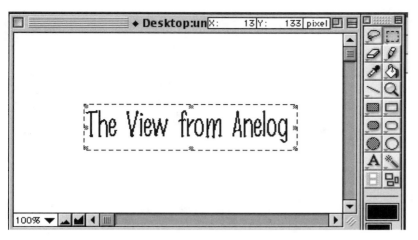

Figure 3.3 Turning text into a picture in a graphics program

Animated GIFS

There's one other kind of graphics file worthy of mention and that's the animated .GIF. You will almost certainly have come across some of these on your journeys across the internet – small animations that briefly amuse and eventually irritate! They are easy enough to create and simply consist of a number of separate frames which are compiled into one .GIF file. Many dedicated web graphics programmes will help you to perform this task but if you want a cheap and cheerful shareware or freeware program you won't do much better than these:

- GIF Construction Set (PC) at http://www.mindworkshop.com/alchemy/legacyapp.html#GCS
- GIF Builder (Mac) at http://macport.sut.ac.jp/soft/grf/

The workings of different animators differ only slightly. A number of small graphic file are created and saved:

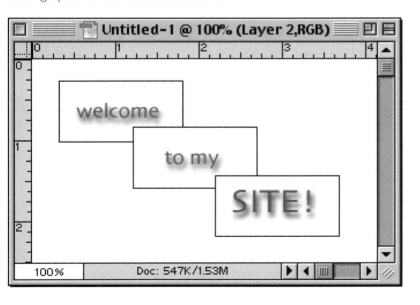

Figure 3.4 Individual graphics files

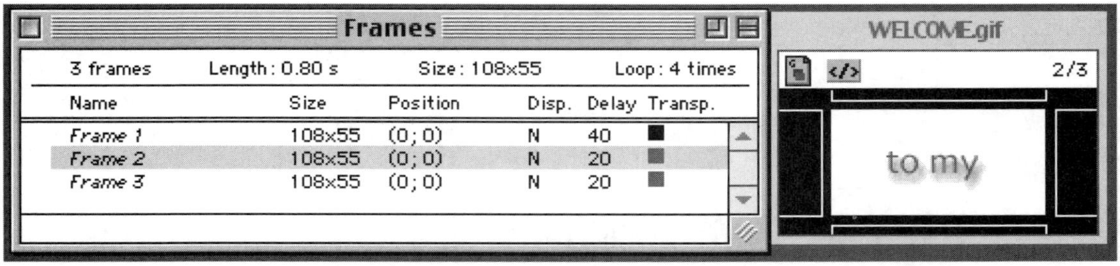

3 frames	Length: 0.80 s		Size: 108x55		Loop: 4 times	
Name	Size	Position	Disp.	Delay	Transp.	
Frame 1	108x55	(0;0)	N	40	■	
Frame 2	108x55	(0;0)	N	20	■	
Frame 3	108x55	(0;0)	N	20	■	

WELCOME.gif   2/3

to my

Figure 3.5 Imported into GifBuilder to create an animation

TIP

One word about animations. They're fun to create and easy to put onto your web page – but don't overdo it!

and then loaded into the animation program (Figure 3.5), where, depending on the program, you can decide how long you want each frame to appear on the screen, whether you want any sort of transitions between frames and so on. The saved animation is called up onto your web page with the same piece of HTML as you'd use for any other .GIF

<IMG SRC="filename.GIF">

216 colours

Before we move on from the subject of graphics perhaps this is the point at which I should tell you just a little more about colour and the Internet. The majority of computers that are likely to gain access to your site are going to be either Apple Macs or PCs. I've already indicated that for the sake of faster downloads it's best to restrict the number of colours you use on your site to 256 – but what I didn't tell you is that, although both Macs and PCs both recognise 256 colours, they don't recognise the same 256 colours. There are, in fact, only 216 that are common to both palettes.

Depending on the graphics package you use, you may find yourself being offered a 'web-safe' palette to work with – if so, use it wherever possible. If you need to work with a colour that isn't one of the lucky 216, your site visitor's browser can either display the colour by 'dithering' (mixing two other colours together), or by substituting some other colour for the one you've chosen. The latter is obviously a fairly unattractive prospect, but dithering is not without its problems either – what may look fine on your machine may look messy, and take a little longer to download on someone else's. This is not to suggest that you should consider yourself to be restricted to the 216 (somewhat lurid) 'web safe' colours, but that you should simply remain aware of the possible consequences or straying too far away from them. As always, take nothing for granted!

Adding links 4

Links manifest themselves in several forms. They might appear on your pages as the familiar underlined blue text, or they might be a picture or some other graphical image. Links are what makes the web what it is. They link your pages together and, equally importantly, they link your site to those of other people – they make you site part of the web. By the way, it's at the point that you start adding links that it becomes really important to have planned your site properly – if you haven't done so already, it's still not too late......

Text links

The simplest way to make a link is to make part of the text a link point – thus clicking on the phrase 'My Music' could take us to a page entitled 'My Music', while clicking on the words 'Home Page' could take us back to the home page. Creating such a link is a very straightforward process in any authoring package, and generally involves highlighting a word or words, clicking on some sort of 'make link' icon, and then steering through the file menus to select the file you want to link to. Coding it yourself is also pretty easy, however, and the HTML for our example above would be:

```
<A HREF="Music.html">My Music</A>.
```

The pattern for any link is always the same – the text held between the <A HREF> and </A> tags acts as the link, while the address that the link will take you to actually sits within the <A HREF> tag itself. That might just be "Music.html" if that page is in the same folder or directory as the page carrying this link, but otherwise you'll need to include the entire path ("Pages/Music.html", for example.)

Picture links

As I've already suggested, it's also possible to use images as links, and here's an example of just such an arrangement, where a graphic image called "button.gif" is used to call up page called "Gigs.html" -

```
<A HREF="Gigs.html"><IMG SRC="button.gif" WIDTH="159" HEIGHT="65"
BORDER="0"></A>
```

It all looks a bit complicated, but in fact most of it will already be familiar to you. You've seen how a text link works and you know how to call up a picture onto your site, and most of this coding is simply achieving these two tasks. You're already aware of the advantage of giving information about the height and width of a picture so the only thing that will be really unfamiliar to you is that BORDER="0" command.. You could type this coding in for yourself if you like, using a graphic file that you already have available, and try experimenting with different numbers for the border. Quite simply, any number other than "0" will place a blue border around your file – the larger the number the larger the border.

Figure 4.1 A button with a border ...
Figure 4.2 ... and without (both work in exactly the same way)

The advantage of having a border is that it makes it very clear to your visitors that the image is a link. The disadvantage is that it can have a negative impact on the overall design of your page. Whether you have a border or not is entirely up to you. For the most part I leave one on when I'm using photographs as links but don't bother when I'm using some other kind of graphic. Anything like the button used in our example above is so obviously waiting for someone to click on it that it doesn't really need the extra hint given by the border.

There are problems concerned with using pictures as links, however, and they largely centre around download times. If you use a picture as a link then it's important to bear in mind that the link will not work until the entire file has downloaded, and if you have a number of such links then it can obviously take some while before your page is functioning properly.

The first way of dealing with this is simply to ensure that all those images used as links are kept as small as possible. The second way of dealing with it is to have two links for each new page, one of which uses an image, while the other uses text. This is a very straightforward process, and one that I've used on my own site. Part of my home page shows a picture of each of my album covers, and each of these images acts as a link that takes the browser to the page relating to that album. Underneath the picture is the title of the album, however, and this has also been linked to the page. This means that visitors to my site don't have to wait until all the images have loaded. If they already know which album they want to look at they just click on the text link.

TIP

Ensure that all the images used as links are kept as small as possible

Anchors

All the links that we've just looked at so far would take the user to the start of the linked page once it had loaded into the browser. It is, however, perfectly possible to create a link that takes the browser to a specific section of a page – and that's any page, including the page that bears the link itself. With web pages that contain a lot of organised text, such as FAQ (Frequently Asked Questions) pages, for instance, it's common practice to have an index at the start of the page that consists of a set of links to other sections of the same page – so the person viewing it can either scroll down the page to reach a particular section, or jump to it directly from the index. On lengthy pages this sometimes manifests itself as a simple listing of all the letters in the alphabet. Clicking on a letter immediately takes the user to those topics starting with that letter.

Creating such a link is a fairly straightforward process but involves just a little extra work, in that you need to put another tag at the point in the page that you want to jump to.

Let's imagine that we need to create one page as a gig list, and let's imagine (chance would be a fine thing) that we've got work booked solid for the next twelve months. A fragment from this page would look something like:

```
July 1st Kings Head, Dudley
July 2nd Scrumpy House, Much Marcle
July 3rd The Lamb, West Malvern
...
```

and so on. This would be a pretty tedious page to scroll down, particularly if we'd got that much work, so at the top of the page we'll put all the months of the year: January, February, March and so on. Now, at the start of the list of July gigs we'd insert this tag

```
<A NAME="July"></A>
```

this is our anchor, and will be invisible to our visitors, because it is all within an HTML tag.

Going back to the top of our page we want to make a link from the word "July" to our July anchor. We do this by writing the following HTML around that word "July":

```
<A HREF="#July">July</A>
```

All the visitor to your site would see would be the "July" between the <A HREF> and </A> tags, but the "#July" would tell the browser to jump to our July anchor point whenever it was clicked on.

It's quite possible to jump to an anchor point on a different page in your site with something like:

Figure 4.3 Graphics *and* text as links

```
<A HREF="Gigs.html#July">These are my July gigs</A>
```

and indeed it's possible to jump to an anchor point on a different site to your own, with something like:

```
<A HREF="http://musicfromthemountains.com/Gigs.html#July">
These are my July gigs</A>
```

but of course the anchor points would already need to be in place since you would have no way of putting them there yourself, given that this was someone else's site you were jumping to.

Thumbnails

There are other kinds of links which are also worth knowing about. One of these involves something called 'thumbnails', whereby a very small image is used as a link to a much larger version of the same picture. In this way, those who want access to the full-sized version can get it, but those who don't only have to wait for the thumbnail to load.

People may well be interested in seeing pictures of you and your band, but they aren't going to be so appreciative of having to wait for several minutes while each of the pictures inches its way onto their screen. If you provide thumbnails you can let your site visitor choose which pictures they want to look at and which ones they want to ignore.

Figure 4.4 Each of these thumbnails will open a larger picture

 This is the view from Anelog looking pretty much due North. On a clear night you can see the lighthouse on Anglesey. The land slopes down to the sea on the left of the picture and here there are dozens of iron age hut rings. You can't see them at all in the summer but in the winter, when the mountain is much more bare, they show up quite distinctly.

Here's a picture looking to the South-West. The pathway beyond the gate winds round towards Uwchmymydd. Get on the road from there and turn right and you'll find the row of cottages that I mentioned on the Lleyn Links page. Keep on going and you'll reach the coastguard's look out post. Go any further and you'll run out of land. You can see Bardsey Island in the far distance in this picture. This is one of a whole series of pictures I took for an album cover - I may use this one at some time.

 This is a very different view of Bardsey, approaching it from the sea on the South Easterly side. There are dozens of seals close to the shore and a feeling of total tranquility. It's a wonderful place to visit on a mild summer's day - I'd imagine it feels a little different in the middle of a gale in February. You have to book several days ahead if you want to visit the island, and then hope that the weather's OK when your day comes!

A word of warning here, however. As we have seen, it's possible to determine the size of an image on a web page simply by specifying its width and height when we bring it onto the page. So, if we have called up an image with a piece of HTML like:

```
<IMG SRC="lleyn2.jpg" WIDTH="365" HEIGHT="244">
```

...it would be possible to produce a much smaller image with something like:

```
<IMG SRC="lleyn2.jpg" WIDTH="183" HEIGHT="122">
```

But in either case the file size would be exactly the same, and so would take exactly the same amount of time to download. The second piece of HTML only determines how the file is displayed after it has been downloaded, and it's that download time that we want to keep to a minimum. The only way to create a proper thumbnail is via your graphics package, which will let you reduce the actual file size and then save it under another name. You would then have two versions of the same picture, one much smaller than the other, and would use the former as a link to the latter.

The HTML for this arrangement would be something like this:

```
<A HREF="fullsize.jpg"><IMG SRC="thumbnail.jpg" ></A>
```

where "thumbnail.jpg" is the image that's displayed on the page but "fullsize.jpg" appears if the thumbnail is clicked on. I've actually removed the WIDTH and HEIGHT tags for the sake of clarity but they should still be included when you're actually trying this:

```
<A HREF="fullsize.jpg"><IMG SRC="thumbnail.jpg" WIDTH="91" HEIGHT="66"></A>
```

You'll notice that the coding only gives the size of the thumbnail, and not the full sized picture, and this is perfectly normal. because only the thumbnail will displayed on the page. The main picture ("fullsize.jpg") will open in a separate, framed window.

Figure 4.5 ... in another window

Image maps

Another way of establishing links – and one that I wouldn't even think of without some sort of authoring package – is by creating what's called a Client Side Image Map. This sounds a little complex but basically involves identifying particular 'hot spots' within an image. each of which serve as links to other pages. Here's an example from a University Department's web site:

Figure 4.6 The Web Page

Clicking on any of the characters in the photograph takes the visitor to that person's personal page. Again, as you can see, there's a second set of text based links for the user who doesn't want to wait for the entire image to load. Certainly a Client Side Image Map is an attractive feature but if you look at some of the HTML that went to create the example above:

```
SHAPE="POLYGON" COORDS="397, 113, 410, 71, 425, 32, 445, 9, 472, 24, 464, 59,
503, 81, 505, 282, 478, 276, 489, 145, 485, 101, 458, 91, 449, 49, 450, 54, 427, 57,
421, 96, 414, 99" HREF="Staff/Frank.html"><AREA SHAPE="POLYGON" COORDS="385,
118, 360, 92, 353, 76, 358, 43, 380, 35, 397, 61, 400, 83, 394, 108, 389, 117"
HREF="Staff/Lesley.html"><AREA SHAPE="POLYGON" COORDS="284, 114, 313, 89, 318,
68, 295, 56, 304, 15, 288, 7, 269, 11, 265, 32, 268, 46, 265, 64, 269, 87, 257, 100"
HREF="Staff/Francis.html">
```

– you can see why I'd rather use an authoring package to create it!

Mail me

One sort of link that's perhaps worth special mention is the email link. If you want your site visitors to send you an email then it's easy enough to insert a piece of text on your page that says something like 'why not email me?' The HTML that would turn the word 'email' into a link that would call up an email page ready addressed to you is simply:

```
why not <A HREF="mailto:mike@musicfromthemountains.com">email </A>me?
```

Where, of course, you'd replace my email address with yours! As always, you're dependent on your visitor and their browser here. If they're using a browser that doesn't support email, or if they haven't configured the preference pages, then they can click for all they are worth, but nothing much will happen! The work round for this, of course, is to ensure that you include your actual email address as well as the link. You might try something like this, which kills two birds with one stone:

```
email me at <A HREF="mailto:mike@musicfromthemountains.com">mike@musicfromthe
mountains.com</A>
```

Links outside

So far I've only talked about links within your own site, but equally important – and straightforward – are links to other peoples'. Typing the following into your page:

```
click <A HREF="http://musicfromthemountains.com">here</A>
```

...would simply display the words 'click here' in a browser window, with the word 'here' highlighted. Clicking on the word 'here', however, would lead someone straight to my web site. (Please feel free to do this, I need all the help I can get!)

If you use a picture as a link to another site then your code might look something like this:

```
<A HREF="http://musicfromthemountains.com"><img src="atb.jpeg" width="65"
height="65"></A>
```

Can you see what's happening?

The only real difference to our previous example is that instead of having a word between the <A HREF> and </A> tags we have a picture (atb.jpeg). It's called up by that <IMG SRC> tag and, to speed up the loading process, you'll see that the image size has also been specified. As you might expect, you can use either .GIFs or JPEGs to make a link.

A couple of things are worth considering when you're making links to other people's sites. Except in specific circumstances it's wisest only to make links to the home page of another site and, once you've done so, it's only courtesy (and good sense) to inform the site owners of the fact – they may well make a link back to your site if you do. Making a link to a page deep within someone else's site (www.musicmtn.demon.co.uk/ tsnaps/snaps/helen.jpg, for example) means that you'll have a dead link on your site the moment they make any change that affects the navigation to that page on theirs.

This raises an interesting point though, and perhaps one that's worth exploring a little. We've already seen the way in which you can include a graphics file on your web site with that <IMG SRC="filename"> tag, and you'll remember that I told you that the "filename" part of the HTML would need to include the path to the graphic if it wasn't held in the same folder as the actual page. We can elaborate on this further. If you wanted to you could put a picture on your own site simply by making a link to that picture on someone else's. So, for example, putting:

```
<IMG SRC="http://musicmtn.demon.co.uk/pictures/mike.jpg"
width="308" height="280" alt="the artist in repose">
```

on your web site would take a picture of me which is on my web site and put it onto yours (go on, why don't you try it – I think I'm ready for cult status of some sort). This trick will work with pretty much any graphic on anyone's site, but it's considered to be a fairly sneaky thing to do without asking their permission, and may very well be a breach of copyright into the bargain.

Many people who suffer this kind of piracy combat it by regularly changing the file names on their own site. They know they've changed the name of "pic1.jpg" to "pic2.jpg", and they've changed their link accordingly. You don't, so all you're left with on your site is a broken link icon!

By the way, you might think there's something a little strange about my address in the link I've just given you. Don't worry about it for now, we'll come to it later.

Targets

A common feature of all the links that you create is that you're able to make some decisions about what will will happen when your visitor clicks on them.

```
<A HREF="chum.html" TARGET="_self">My Best Chum</A>
```

...will open that "My Best Chum" page in place of the current page. This is probably what you'll want while visitors are navigating around your site, and is how most browsers will respond if they are given no TARGET information. This, on the other hand:

```
<A HREF="chum.html" TARGET="_blank">My Best Chum</A>
```

...will open the 'My Best Chum' page in a new window in the browser, leaving the existing page still open in the window behind it. The advantage of this is that the user is more likely to return to that first page since it's still actually sitting on their computer – a point worth considering when you're setting up links to other people's sites.

Link philosophy

It might also be worth considering exactly what rationale you'll use for creating links to other sites. It's your site after all, and there's nothing stopping you creating links to 'my favourite football team', 'my favourite film', 'my favourite hamburger joint' and so on ad infinitum. It's just worth wondering how many people actually follow those links, and why they should want to follow them. Think about why they visit your site and what would have attracted them to it. Then think about links that relate to that attraction.

My first couple of albums, for example, relate to the Lleyn Peninsula of North Wales. On the pages relating to those albums I've established as many links to interesting sites devoted to North Wales as I can find. On the page for my most recent album *Compositions of Stone* (shameless plug) I've presented links to a variety of excellent sites dedicated to Standing Stones, Stone Circles and Alignments of Stone – and so it goes on.

Home page links

Before we finish looking at links (at least for now) there's one more thing worth bearing in mind. The bigger your site becomes the more complex it's going to be, and the easier it will be to get lost in it. Don't turn your site into a mystery tour (unless that's your actual intention) because you want to hold your visitor's attention. Whatever else you do be sure to provide lots of links back to your home page. Ideally they should be in the same position on every page, and they should look the same. Make it obvious. If you provide an eccentric navigation system that's difficult to follow your visitors are likely to become frustrated and vote with their feet. Or, at least, their mouse!

5 So far, so good!

What you know so far

Let's put together everything we've learnt so far, and see what sense we can make of it all. Have a look at the following piece of code and see if you can understand what's going on

```
<HTML>
<HEAD><TITLE>The View from Anelog</TITLE></HEAD>
<BODY background="pictures/parchmnt.jpg">
<P><CENTER><IMG SRC="vfatitl.GIF" WIDTH=294 HEIGHT=51>
<HR></CENTER></P>
<P><IMG SRC="Covers/vfa.jpeg" WIDTH=151 HEIGHT=232 ALIGN=LEFT>
<I><FONT size="4">Mount Anelog is a small mountain on the furthest tip of the Lleyn
peninsula of Wales. To the South-West it overlooks Bardsey Island, a place of pilgrimage since
the 5th Century. The music on this tape was largely written and recorded on the mountain. It
reflects its peace and tranquillity – and its mystery.</FONT></I> </P>
<P><B><FONT color="#990000">Track Titles</FONT> -</B> The View from Anelog.
Night. Sky from Mynydd Mawr. Our Footprints on the Sands – Porth Oer. Evening Braich Anelog.
St Mary's Well. Bardsey Island. Footsteps on the Mountain. Twenty Thousand Saints. Gulls'
Flight: Early Evening, Waiting for Daybreak. <B>Available as cassette only.</B> </P>
<P>To order click <A HREF="order.html">here</A></P>
<P>If you'd like to look at a range of links to various sites on the Lleyn Peninsula you could try
<A HREF="Lynlnk.html" target="_blank">here</A> </P>
<P><FONT size="2">You can email me at <A HREF="mailto:mike@musicfromthemountains.
com">mike@musicfromthemountains.com</A></FONT></P>
<HR>
</BODY>
</HTML>
```

So what did you make of it?

This is a web page taken from my very first web site and, given that it was almost the first page that I wrote, it's comparatively simple to follow – though it may still look pretty confusing at first glance.

The page is advertising the first of my albums and you'll see the name of that album – *The View from Anelog* placed between the <TITLE> tags so that it will show up on the browser's title bar. You'll also see that I've got a tiled background, and that the tile I'm using is called "parchmnt.jpg" and that it's located in a folder called "pictures"

The heading for the page is a GIF with the pithy name of "vfatitl.GIF", and it's centred on the page. (You remember I talked about using head-

So far, so good! What you know so far

39

ings made with a Marker Fine Point font when we were talking about graphics? This is one of those headings)

Now you'll see an <HR> tag which we haven't yet covered. We'll come back to that in a little while but before we do you'll see another image being called up with that <IMG SRC> tag and that the image aligned to the left. This is a picture of the album cover (from way back in the days when people bought tapes) and all the text is going to flow down its right hand side.

The text itself is pretty straightforward. You'll see FONT sizes being called up, you'll see text being emboldened and italicised and you'll see the words "track Titles" being turned red. The text is broken into paragraphs with the <P> tag.

You'll then see some links to other pages – both of which are in the same folder as the one we're looking at and the second of which will call up a new window when it's clicked on (target ="_blank"). Finally we have an email link. This is what it all looks like when viewed in a browser.

TIP

Be sure to provide lots of links back to your home page

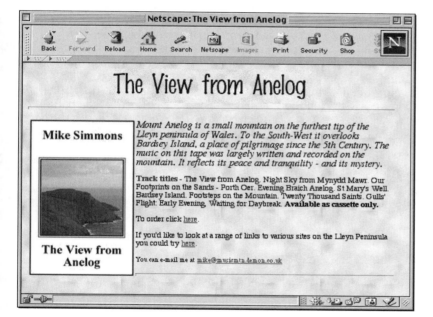

Figure 5.1 Shameless plug!

Horizontal rule

So what about that <HR> tag, you'll be asking.

HR stands for "horizontal rule" and you'll see the effect it has near the top and bottom of the picture above – a line running (horizontally!) across the page. You might like to play around with this a little. Open up one of the example pages you've been working on and just type the <HR> tag somewhere between the <BODY> tags and when you look at the page in a browser you'll see a horizontal line stretching across the page. You can edit the width and thickness of this line in a variety of ways. For example typing <HR SIZE="20"> would create a very much thicker line. Alternatively, typing <HR WIDTH="75%"> would produce a line which would always be 75 percent of the width of the browser page, while <HR WIDTH="75"> would produce a line 75 pixels long regardless of the page width.

This actually introduces an important concept in HTML: the difference between relative sizes or dimensions and absolute ones. Relative sizes mean that whatever size you choose will always fit into the window in which a browser is displaying your page (since they are defined in terms of fractions of the size of that window). Specifying an absolute size, on the other hand, may mean that the browser can't display the whole line within the window (forcing the person viewing the page to either enlarge the window or scroll around the page), but allows for a greater degree of precision – it's simply a matter of deciding which is most appropriate in each case. In case you were wondering, it's perfectly acceptable to combine these attributes, so that:

```
<HR WIDTH="50%" size="10">
```

would create a thick line that was half the width of the page.

There are, of course, a thousand variations on this theme! As you will have probably realised, by the way, the <HR> tag exists *without* an </HR> closer.

Another – and more colourful – way of breaking up text on your page is to use an image instead of the <HR> tag. As we've already seen, as soon as you start introducing images on your web site it's important to keep file sizes in mind but, given the size of the average line this is unlikely to be too much of a problem. However, f you're content for your line to be a single colour then there's one trick you might like to try which will reduce the size of your file to an absolute minimum. You'll remember that on page 33 I showed you that we could dictate the size at which an image was actually displayed on a web page quite regardless of the actual size of the image itself. This can work in our favour. It's quite possible to create an image no more than a pixel square but to call it up with the following code:

> **TIP**
>
> *If you want to see the source code of a web page you're viewing, simply select 'source' or 'page source' from the 'View' menu*

```
<P ALIGN="CENTER"><IMG SRC="dot.gif" WIDTH="400" HEIGHT="8"> </P>
```

and produce a thick coloured line running neatly across the centre of the page – it must be magic!

If you'd like real examples of how HTML coding is used, and you already have Internet access, then the world is essentially your oyster, since both Internet Explorer and Navigator will allow you to view any web page as 'source' code enabling you to see how it's made up. Simply go to the page you're interested in, select 'source' or 'page source' from the 'View' menu, and the full text, including HTML tags, is displayed for you to study, save or print out.

Tables and frames 6

So it looks like you've got a pretty good understanding of most of the bare bones of HTML coding. You know how to create a page, you know how to bring pictures onto that page, and you know how to link that page to others. You also know how to get text to go roughly where you want it to go, but you may also have found that some of your attempts to lay out your pages exactly as you wanted them were more than a little frustrating.

Yes, you can decide whether the text runs to the left or right of a picture, but what if you want an image, then some text, then another image, and then more text – all running on the same line? With the HTML that we've already looked at this degree of control would be impossible. Luckily help is at hand, in the form of tables.

Tables

A table is essentially a rectangular matrix of cells which can be made to fill a page, or part of one – or, indeed, to fill a cell in another table. You can put pictures or text into each of these cells and you can determine their position within that cell. You can also leave any cell blank if you want to. You can also combine cells.

Why you should want to do all this might seem a little unclear at the moment, but in point of fact the table is a very powerful piece of HTML and offers a level of control over the layout of your pages which has, up until now, been impossible. The downside of all this is that constructing tables is quite a complex process and requires a very clear head!

Certainly tables can be constructed without using authoring software but the larger the table the easier it can be to make a slip in your coding – and the harder it can be to find that slip.

<TR> and <TD> tags

With a fairly simple table the HTML is pretty straightforward, however. Take a look at this piece of code:

```
<TABLE BORDER="3">
<TR> <TD>text</TD> <TD>more text</TD> <TD>yet more</TD> </TR>
<TR> <TD>even more</TD> <TD>much more</TD> <TD>no more</TD> </TR>
</TABLE>
```

which, located between the <BODY> tags, is all the code you need to produce a basic HTML table. And this is what it would look like:

Figure 6.1 A tiny table!

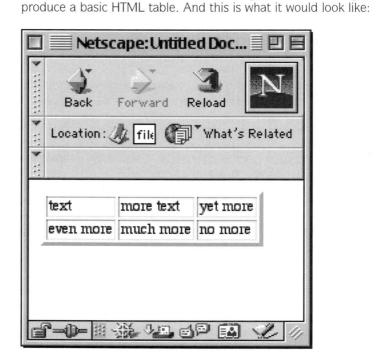

First we see the <TABLE> tag which, fairly reasonably, informs the browser that what follows is a table. (Don't worry about the "BORDER" part of the tag, we'll come back to that in just a moment.) The <TR> tag announces the start of a row, and then the <TD> tags indicate a piece of data to be inserted into a cell. Each pair of <TD> and </TD> tags announce the presence of another cell in that first row until the row is ended by a </TR> tag and another row is started with the next <TR> tag, and so it goes on.

More table tags

At it's most basic, that's all it takes to put together a table – the browser will automatically decide how large each cell needs to be, and adjust it accordingly – but if you have a look at the following code, and the page it produces, you'll see that it's possible to create something much more complex.

```
<TABLE WIDTH="75%" BORDER="3" BGCOLOR="#CCCCFF" CELLPADDING="5"
CELLSPACING="4" BORDERCOLOR="#0000FF">
<TR>
<TD COLSPAN="2" BGCOLOR="#FF0033" ALIGN="CENTER">text </TD>
<TD WIDTH="60%">more text</TD> </TR>
<TR>
<TD ROWSPAN="2" WIDTH="15%" VALIGN="top"><FONT COLOR="#FF0033">
<IMG SRC="helen.JPG" WIDTH="65" HEIGHT="92"></FONT>
</TD>
<TD WIDTH="25%"> much more</TD>
<TD WIDTH="60%" BGCOLOR="#0000FF"><FONT COLOR="#FFF423"> even
more</FONT></TD>
</TR>
<TR> <TD WIDTH="25%" VALIGN="TOP">yet more</TD> <TD WIDTH="60%"
VALIGN="BOTTOM"> <DIV ALIGN="RIGHT">no more</DIV> </TD>
</TR> </TABLE>
```

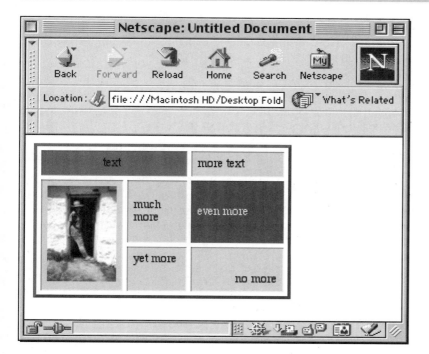

Figure 6.2 The Web Page

Let's see what's happening. First we have a declaration that the table
will occupy 75 percent of the width of the browser page.

- BORDER tells the browser how wide the border of the table should be
- BGCOLOR determines the background colour of the entire table.
- CELLPADDING determines the space between the content of the cell and the cell wall
- CELLSPACING determines the space between individual cells. Finally
- BORDERCOLOR specifies that the entire table will have a coloured border "#0000FF"

Note that all of this information is contained within that initial <TABLE> tag and dictates the common attributes of the entire table.

COLSPAN, ALIGN and ROWSPAN tags

The <TD> tag you'll be familiar with, but this time there's rather more information to digest. We see that the first cell will span two columns (COLSPAN = "2"), that the background colour for that particular cell is #FF0033 – a shade of red – and that the text within that cell is centred. Notice too that the background colour information which was set within the <TABLE> tag is being overridden by the information for this particular cell – you can think of the <TABLE> tag information as simply being a set of default values, many of which can be overridden at a later point in the coding.

The <ALIGN> tag determines the horizontal alignment of the text – alternatives would have been "left" and, you've guessed it, "right". We've already seen what COLSPAN does so it won't be any surprise to see that ROWSPAN tells the browser that the cell will span two rows. VALIGN="TOP" dictates the position of the text within the cell, but this time across a vertical axis – the alternatives would have been "middle" or "bottom".

Your best bet, as ever, is simply to experiment until you've got a real understanding of what's going on. Change the tags and look at the result in the browser. (Can't see any difference? Did you remember to click on reload/refresh?) Change the tags again, and go back to the browser once more. Just remember that every cell can be configured in any way that you want it to be. You can choose the background colour, the colour of the text, the alignment of the text, the size of the cell and its relationship with other cells.

And, as you can see by that <IMG SRC="helen.JPG"> tag, you can include pictures in a cell too.

What all this means, of course, is that you can position text or graphics anywhere on the page with a degree of precision that would otherwise seem impossible. But at a price, you might say – the price being that the whole thing needs to be included within a visible framework, which will inevitably introduce restrictions as far as the aesthetics of your design are concerned.

Not so. Have a look at this page from my web site (Figure 6.3). You'll see that all the information – text, pictures and links – is, quite obviously, contained within a table. But it's only obvious because I like that particular effect. Now take a look at Figure 6.4

Exactly the same arrangement of text and graphics, but no apparent sign of a table – yet that's still exactly what it is. All the information you see displayed is still set between a pair of <TABLE> tags. The difference in appearance between these two screens all comes down to that <TABLE BORDER> tag which I mentioned just a few paragraphs ago. On the first page the table border tag has a value of 1, which makes the framework apparent, while on the second there's a value of 0, which makes it invisible – it's as easy as that. What happens if it has a value of 2? Or 10? Give it a try!

One final thing about tables, if you want a completely empty cell you'll find that some browsers present them as being "filled in" – you can get round this simply by putting a
 tag between the relevant <TD> and </TD> tags.

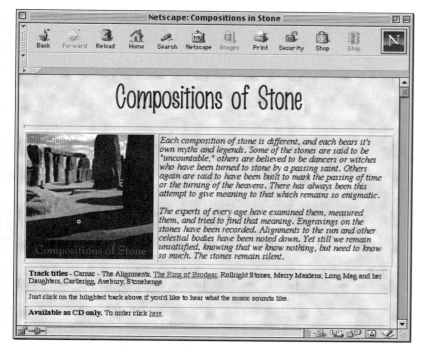

Figure 6.3 BORDER = 1

and ...

Figure 6.4 BORDER = 0

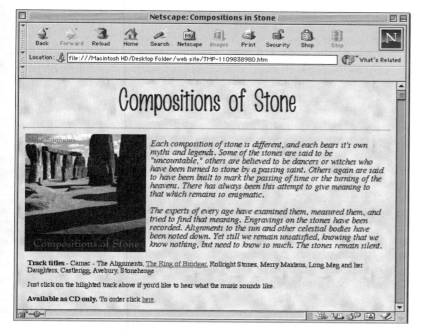

You've now got all the information you need to create a perfectly good web site. You know how to change the size and colour of your text, you know how to create links and you know how to bring pictures onto a page. Until a very few years ago this wasn't simply all you needed to know, it was pretty much all there *was* to know. Things have moved on, however, and so far we're really only scratching at the surface. You could stop here if you wanted to – but you ain't seen nothing yet!

Frames

One of the difficulties with the kind of arrangement we've looked at so far is that with all but the smallest of sites navigation can become pretty tedious.

Let me take you back to my very first web site. On the home page I had a thumbnail of each of my albums. Clicking on the thumbnail took the visitor to the page relating to that album. It did this with the default TARGET="_SELF" command so that the new page opened in the place of the home page. Once a visitor had read the text on the page, and listened to the music there (I thought that might interest you – we'll come to it a little later!), they had to click on the "back" button on the browser to go back to the home page before they could select another album. Not very elegant. I could have used TARGET="BLANK", of course, but that would only mean that the album information would open in a new window which would itself have to be closed before the visitor could even see the home page again.

Another alternative would have been to have all the links to all the albums on every page. A possibility in my case, but what if I had 20 or 30 albums – there'd be so so many links on each page that there would barely be room for any new information! What I'm leading up to here is something called Frames, a very elegant solution to the problem, and one that is in very common usage.

The core to the concept is that the user's browser is split into two or more windows, each of which can contain an individual web page. This in itself might seem fairly pointless but, if I tell you that HTML coding will allow you determine what appears in one window when someone clicks on a link in another, then you may begin to see the point of the exercise. Though it's quite possible to have more than a dozen frames on the screen at the same time, the most common arrangement is simply to have two. One of these remains static, and simply carries all the links to the main areas of the site. Clicking on one of these links calls up the content in the other frame. This means that it's possible to navigate from place to place on the site without constantly having to go back to the home page.

The "links" frame can be on the left hand side of the browser, the right, the top or the bottom – it's up to you. On my own site I've arranged things so that one frame runs down the left hand side of my page and carries little more than a row of thumbnails of all my album covers. Clicking on one of the thumbnails displays details of that album in the other frame via a series of links I created. This allows people to jump from album to album with the minimum of fuss. As well as the album thumbnails there's also a button which links back to the home page, so that visitors can return to that point if they wish to.

So, how do we go about it?

The pages in a "framed" web site are written in exactly the same way as we've already discussed – in fact, they can be pages that you've already written. The one extra component you need to write is something called a frame holder, which is simply an extra page carrying a chunk of HTML which determines exactly how the browser is going to be divided up. Have a look at this:

```
<HTML>
<TITLE>This is the only title anyone visiting a framed site will see</TITLE>
<FRAMESET COLS=50%,50%>
<FRAME NAME="framea" SRC="pagea.html">
<FRAME NAME="frameb" SRC="pageb.html">
</FRAMESET>
</HTML>
```

This simple piece of HTML is all you really need to know if you're going to get to grips with frames. Let me talk you through what's happening. First of all I've included the <TITLE> tags and the message you'll see between them is worth bearing in mind. The text between the <TITLE> tags on the "frameholder" page is the only text that will appear on the browser TITLE bar, regardless of what page your visitor is looking at. On my site I've made that universal title the name of my company – "Music from the Mountains" – but you might want to use the name of your band, your own name, or whatever would be most appropriate.

The next tag, <FRAMESET COLS>, tells the browser that the window is going to be divided up into two columns (as opposed to rows), and those 50% marks indicate that each column will be of equal width. (I think you've got a pretty good idea of what might happen if you change the figures to 20% and 80%, by why not give it a try?)

The two <FRAME> lines give further information about each frame. The left hand column – the first one we read about – is named "framea" and the browser is instructed to fill that frame with a page called "pagea.html". The second column is rather excitingly called "frameb" and will display the page called "pageb.html".

Naming frames

The names given to the frames, and to the pages that fill them, are entirely up to you. I've used "a" and "b" for convenience but there's no significance in that – as long as you do name them, they can be called whatever you want.

It's probably fractionally easier if the content pages are written before the frame holder page that's going to hold them, but it really makes very little difference. You can go on editing the content pages whenever you want, and the changes that you make will become apparent next time the frame holder page is opened up in a browser.

If you'd like to break your page up into rows instead of columns then I think you can probably guess what would happen if you replace our

```
<FRAMESET COLS=50%,50%>
```

with this:

```
<FRAMESET ROWS="25%,75%">
```

Yes indeed, two rows running across your browser, the first occupying 25 percent of the space, the other 75 percent.

You don't have to stop there, though; you can create frames within frames within frames if you want to, though the more you add, the messier things are likely to become – if you have a look at Figure 6.5 I think you'll see what I mean!

Figure 6.5 Very very messy!

and this is the HTML that went to produce it!

```
<FRAMESET COLS="286,286">
<FRAMESET COLS="141,142">
<FRAMESET ROWS="240,241">
<FRAME SRC="vfa.html">
<FRAME SRC="stone.html">
</FRAMESET>
<FRAME SRC="doa.html">
</FRAMESET>
<FRAMESET ROWS="240,241">
<FRAMESET COLS="141,142">
<FRAME SRC="ftb.html">
<FRAME SRC="audram.html">
</FRAMESET>
<FRAME SRC="intro.html">
</FRAMESET>
</FRAMESET>
```

So far we've only used relative terms to describe the size of our columns and rows, but you can equally well use absolute dimensions. Replacing our <FRAMESET> tag with something like:

```
<FRAMESET COLS=50,500>
```

would produce two columns, the first 50 pixels wide, the other 500. There are some problems inherent in this arrangement, however, and they largely centre around the fact that not every monitor is the same size, and not every user opens up their browser to the full width of the screen. Using absolute dimensions could mean that a great deal of your page vanishes off the screen, and will only return by the regular use of scroll bars. The way round this is to use something like the following code:

```
<FRAMESET COLS="20,*">
```

From this we see that the first column is defined absolutely, at 20 pixels, while the * symbol indicates that the rest of the available space, be it 80 or 800 pixels, is all allocated to the other column. This is particularly useful if you're using one column as a menu. since, if all the items on your menu page are only 20 pixels wide, then you simply don't need the frame that holds it to be much wider that that, regardless of how large the entire browser window is.

Once you've sorted out the relative sizes of your frames there's very little else to do. You don't enter any text, sound or graphics into this page because what you've created is simply a page which will hold other pages, and it's those pages which your visitors will see when they visit your site. To take a small detour here, most ISPs expect you to name your home page, the page that all other pages link from, with something like 'index.html'. If you're going to use frames on your site then it's the page that holds the other pages – i.e. the "frameholder" – that gets given the designated name.

INFO

The real power of a frame set, as I've indicated earlier, is that it enables you to produce a much more friendly navigation system than would otherwise be possible.

You will have noticed earlier on that we didn't simply determine the size of our frames, we also gave them names. We did this so that we could use them as part of our navigation.

An example from my site reads something like this:

```
<FRAME SRC="Albms.html" NAME="framea">
<FRAME SRC="intro.html" NAME="frameb">
```

"What's this?" you're probably asking, "last time it was FRAME NAME and then SRC, this time it's FRAME SRC and then NAME. What's happening?" A good question, and one that raises a point that's worth looking into a little more thoroughly. What we've really got here is a <FRAME> tag which has been extended by including both NAME and SRC information within it. The order of these extras doesn't actually matter, all that matters is that the actual syntax is correct. This won't be the only time that you come across this sort of anomaly, so if you come across another piece of coding that seems to be in the wrong order, don't worry – if it works, it isn't!

So back to our example, you'll see that I've stuck with the same frame names – "framea" and "frameb" – and put a page called "Albms.html" into "framea", and a page called "intro.html" into "frameb". Having done this, I can start establishing links between the frames. Here's an example of a link that's on my 'Albms.html' page:

```
<A HREF="stone.html" TARGET="frameb">Compositions of
Stone</A>
```

What we see here is a straightforward link from the words "Compositions of Stone" which is targeted to the frame named "frameb". This means that when these words are clicked, the page 'stone.html' will appear in the frame named "frameb" instead of "intro.html".

Figure 6.6 Before clicking on one of the links

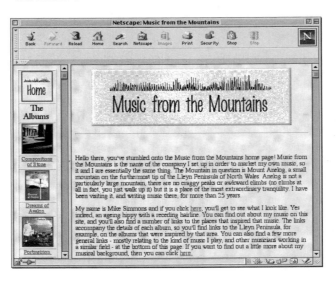

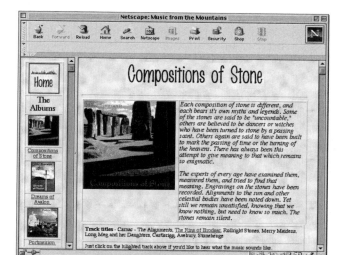

Figure 6.7 ... and afterwards

As we've already seen, you can have as many frames as you need (but no more than you need, please!) and, as long as you name each one of them, your links can make any page appear wherever you want it to. How do you make a page appear in the same page as the link? Simply exclude any target data, since the HTML default is simply to replace the link page with the new one.

One of the less attractive features of a frames system is that you can end up with an awful lot of scroll bars on your site. You can avoid this by including

```
SCROLLING = "NO"
```

within the <FRAME> tags like this:

```
<FRAME SRC="Albmfr.html" NAME="framea" SCROLLING="NO">
```

This will suppress scroll bars on an individual frame, while putting the same command within the <FRAMESET> tags suppresses all the scroll bars on all the frames on a page.

You need to be very careful here, however, since not everybody's monitor is going to be the same size as yours.

Remember, HTML is not desktop publishing, it's a mark-up language, and if a visitor to your site has configured their browser to display body text at a larger point size, or in a smaller window, or if they've simply got a smaller monitor than you, then they're inevitably going to wind up feeling pretty frustrated.

A safer alternative would be as follows:

> ### INFO
>
> *Just because you can see all the text in a frame on your machine doesn't mean that everybody else will.*

```
<FRAME SRC="Albmfr.html" NAME="framea" SCROLLING="AUTO">
```

where scroll bars will be permitted, but only if they are needed. So, if an individual page's content is small enough not to need them then your visitor's browser won't provide them. However, once there is any data outside a frame then they will appear.

You're on safer ground using SCROLLING = "NO" If you have a frame that simply carries a graphic, like the 'module' navigation bar on the SOS web site, for example, that you can be sure is smaller than the smallest browser window that any of your visitors are likely to use.

Figure 6.7 You can see that the "module" is placed hard to the left, for added safety

You can, in fact disguise the fact that there's a frame there entirely by using the following piece of code within the FRAMESET tag:

```
FRAMEBORDER="0" FRAMESPACING="0" BORDER="0"
```

Take a look at the following page from PC Publishing – it's actually made up of three different frames, though you might not know it unless you looked at the code.

As always, it's down to some judicious experimentation, coupled with careful analysis of the source code on other people's web sites – it there for you to have a look at, so why not check what other people have done?

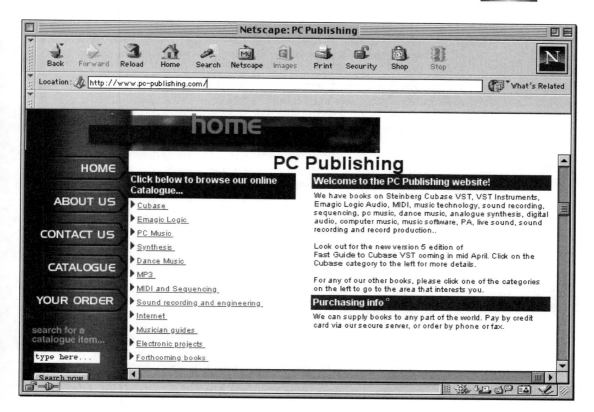

Figure 6.9 Three frames – but would you know it?

Wot, no frames?

Though frames have become extremely common over the last two or three years there are still people out there who, for one reason or another, are using browsers which do not support them. The most basic way of dealing with this is to include something like the following below the </FRAMESET> tag on your frameholder page:

```
<NOFRAMES>
<BODY>Sorry, your browser doesn't support frames so you're not going to be able to visit this site! </BODY>
</NOFRAMES>
```

To make it a little more friendly you could include a link to the browser upgrade page of your choice or, if you really want to make sure that you reach as many as people as possible, you could include a link to an unframed version of your site. This doesn't involve you in half as much work as you might think, and generally comes down to creating a new home page (which will not be called index.html) and then sorting out an unframed navigation system which will allow your visitor to reach all the other pages you have created.

As I've already said, one of the features of HTML that it's important to be aware of is that if a browser doesn't recognise something it will simply ignore it. So, if you spell a tag incorrectly it will be disregarded,

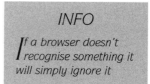

INFO

If a browser doesn't recognise something it will simply ignore it

and if your framed site is visited by a 'no frames' browser it will simply display a plain grey page – so at least get a <NOFRAMES> message up there so your potential visitor knows what's happening!

You've been framed

A word of warning about frames. I recently received an email from someone who had visited my site and found the menu bar missing. I checked it on my machine, I checked it on several others, and the menu bar was, as always, there. Further exploration revealed that my visitor had forgotten the name of my site and simply done a search for 'Music from the Mountains' in one of the search engines.

Search engines index the contents of all the pages of a site, not just the home page, and the first page that this engine came up with happened to be the introduction, which was what came up on my visitor's browser – and which had no links on it, since the idea is that visitors use the navigation panel to get around the site.

As we've just seen, the introduction and the navigation panel are different pages, which are supposed to be held in different frames – but going direct to the introduction bypassed the index page which set up the frames. Without that setup, it was impossible to navigate anywhere else in the site.

The workaround? I've just created a small 'home page' link at the very bottom of every page, which will take visitors back to 'index.html'. Most people will never use it, most people will probably never even see it, but the next person who wanders 'sideways' into my site via a search engine will be able to use that button to get into the rest of my site.

Testing, testing, one, two, three

If you've been steadily working your way through this book, and haven't simply stumbled onto this page in a book shop somewhere (buy the book, it'll make you rich and famous and hugely attractive) you should have a pretty good understanding of the basics of HTML by now. If you haven't started already, I'd say that this was probably the time to start working more seriously on creating your own site. As soon as you make this transition between learning HTML and actually writing it, however, you must maintain a constant awareness of the importance of testing your work.

The two most popular browsers are Internet Explorer and Netscape Navigator and you should have copies of both programmes on your computer so that you can see what your site will look like on each of them. You can't bank on them being the same, though they generally will look pretty similar. Likewise, if you're writing your site on a Mac you need to check what it will look like on a PC, and vice versa. If you know someone who works from a different platform to your own then copy your site onto a Zip disk or whatever and pay them a visit. It's when you start viewing your work on other people's machines that you realise that HTML is not a precise science, and you really need to cover your bases as well as you're able. There's nothing more distressing than getting your site up onto the Internet only to find that most people who visit it are only presented with a garbled version of your creation.

Things become more complicated when we consider that both browsers have gone through a number of incarnations. It would be unreasonable to expect you to have a copy of every version of every browser but do bear in mind that not everybody upgrades, and unless you're happy to cut out great swathes of the surfing public you really need to keep an awareness of how your site is going to look in as many situations as you possibly can.

I recently created a web site for a university department and was able to install it on the local server before publishing to the Internet. Having done this I walked from room to room viewing it on different people's machines. I wasn't expecting total uniformity, because I knew that various staff members had configured their preference pages to their own tastes, and not everybody had the same version of browser. What I hadn't bargained for was the way in which some machines would tolerate any anomalies in my coding while others wouldn't stand for it at all. An odd extra </TR> tag which had been ignored by my own machine and browser caused absolute havoc on someone else's. The obvious lesson is to be scrupulous in your coding – and check that everything's OK on every machine you bump into.

Putting music on your site 8

This, of course, is what you've been waiting for. Given that you're reading this book your site is very likely to be about music in some way. It might be your music, it might be someone else's, but if you're going to tell people about that music, and maybe show them what the musicians who made it look like, then it seems reasonable enough that you should also want to give them the opportunity of hearing what that music sounds like. Surprising as it may seem this is, in fact, very easily done, and requires no more than this simple piece of HTML:

```
<A HREF="filename.wav">you can hear some music here</A>
```

This will enable those of your visitors with a compatible browser – which would, in fact, be pretty much everyone – to hear any sound file which has been saved in the .WAV format at the click of a mouse. Saving your music in this format is straightforward enough, and there are a number of commercial and shareware programmes that will perform the task with the greatest of ease.

However, if you have a feeling that this is all just a bit too good to be true, then you're absolutely right. The problem, once again, is all down to file size. When we talked about including pictures on your site, I stressed that the bigger the file is, the longer it will take for it to download. Well, it's just the same with sound – but if pictures are big, then uncompressed audio files (such as WAVs and AIFFs) are simply enormous, taking up approximately 90K per second of sound in mono! Even with quite a short file, you're likely to lose a few visitors who'll simply give up on the sheer tedium of waiting for the thing to download before they can start listening to it. The .WAV file can be worth using, but if you want to showcase your music – which, in my opinion, must mean a clip of at least 30 seconds – you're going to need to look elsewhere.

So what can be done? You'll have noticed back then that I said that uncompressed sound files are enormous, and it is this qualifier that is significant. Though there was a time when using WAV files (along with the older AU files) was the only way in which we could get sound onto our sites, some rather more attractive alternatives are now available. But at at price!

INFO

If pictures are big, then uncompressed audio files (such as WAVs and AIFFs) are simply enormous

Plug in for sound!

The last few years have seen an ongoing battle between Internet Explorer and Netscape for supremacy over the web, each striving to outdo the other in the facilities that they provide. This has partly been achieved by upgrades in the coding of the browsers themselves, partly by the use of 'helper' applications, and partly by the development of plug-in technology.

Helpers and plug-ins

Helper applications are small subsidiary programs which are called up by the browser when they are confronted by a particular file type, and asked to handle that file. The Quicktime Movie Player, for example, might be called up whenever the browser is confronted (reasonably enough) by a Quicktime movie.

Plug-ins, on the other hand, are small programs which, when installed, extend the browser's functionality – in just the same way as plug-in effects add to the capabilities of a program like Logic Audio, or plug in filters can be used to enhance Photoshop.

The chief difference as far as the end user is concerned is that plug-ins tend to be rather more transparent than do helper applications. If your browser has been installed with the Shockwave plug-in, for example, you probably won't even know when it's in use. If you should visit a "Shocked" site without that plug-in, however, then it's lack will be immediately apparent, since you won't be able to view the page in the way the designer intended – and the only way of doing so would be to download the plug-in and install it on your system.

Figure 8.1 Internet Explorer offers to find you a plug-in

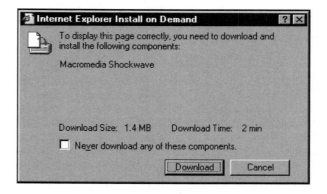

Over the last few years a lot of work has been done to find ways of compressing audio files sufficiently to make them a viable proposition to the web, and now no-one would really recommend using .WAV files except possibly for very short clips of sound. However, the difficulty with all these new formats is that, without exception, they rely on your site visitor having some sort of plug-in or helper application installed on their computer.

The problem with this is that research has shown that the one thing web users hate above all else is having to leave a site to download some plug-in or helper application that they don't already have installed. In fact most people don't even bother, they just move onto another site. What this means is that you must encode your audio files to a format that will be playable by the majority of your visitors without forcing them to first leave your site. In other words, you need to go for one of the major players – the most popular encoding systems that most people's browsers will already be configured for.

So who are the major players? MP3 and RealAudio are the names that immediately spring to mind, with Quicktime coming up close behind. We'll be looking at each of these formats over the next few pages, looking at their strengths and weaknesses and the ways in which you can utilise them on your site. The good news is that you don't have to commit yourself to any one format. As long as you've been allocated enough space on your ISP's server there's nothing stopping you from encoding your music in as many ways as you can think of – and thus ensuring that you hang on to as many visitors as possible.

To stream or not to stream

Essentially, there are two ways of putting music on to your web site. One is to produce files that can be downloaded and played back by the user at a later date: the other is to provide files which will play while they are actually downloading, in a system known as streaming.

The advantage of this kind of arrangement is twofold. Firstly, the end user is less likely to become bored by the wait and give up, and second-ly, they're much more likely to click on something 'just to see what it sounds like' if they're able to hear the music straight away, rather than having to wait. I use a streaming system on my site and I sell music on the strength of what people hear. I doubt if my sales would be half what they are if all I offered was a group of WAV files.

The problem with any streaming system is that it will always require the sound file to be heavily compressed. The more you think about it the more logical this becomes. The entire file doesn't need to be down-loaded before it starts playing but, once it does start, there's a kind of conveyor belt operating. Some of the data is downloaded and it starts playing – and then the next piece of data needs to be downloaded – and be ready to play – before the first piece finishes, and so it goes on. If there's a break in the conveyor belt then the music won't play continu-ously and there will be a pause until the next package of data is deliv-ered. The trick with streaming audio is to try to make the file small enough so that those pauses do not occur.

Compression

The trade-off here comes in the quality of the sound being reproduced. CD-quality digital audio consists of two channels of 16-bit, 44.1kHz sound. This means that a CD player has to access the data which is con-verted into this sound at a rate of 2 x 16 x 44100 bits per second – something like 1411 kilobits per second. The fastest modem currently on the market will handle just 56 kilobits per second – and even this is just a theoretical maximum possible transfer rate – so it's clear that a great deal of compression is going to have to take place.

All the sound formats that we'll be looking at involve data compression of some kind, whereby data that we can do without is discarded, and that which we need is retained, but streaming requires the greatest compres-sion of all, with an inevitable loss of quality. The greater the compression, the smaller the file will become, but the more degraded the quality of the sound is likely to be (in the same way as heavily data-compressed JPEG files are smaller than lightly compressed ones, but look worse).

The problem with compression is not unique to streaming, however, it's just more obvious. The computer world is currently witnessing a tussle between a number of major players who are striving to come up with the best possible system of compression – i.e. one that produces the best compromise between file size and audio quality – and to get it adopted as an industry standard. At the moment there is no such standard, which means that any musician wanting to put music onto their site has to ask themselves a number of crucial questions.

- What speed modem are visitors to the site most likely to have?
- What plug-ins or players are they most likely to already have installed on their computer?
- What compression system is currently performing the most effective balancing act between speed and quality?
- Am I prepared to pay to license an encoding system?

A lot of questions here. And here's another one for you – why do you want to put music on your site? You'd probably respond to this by saying that you want people to listen to it, and I'd respond with another question – so why do you want them to listen to it? Let me explain. Before you can decide what encoding system – or systems – you're going to use you need to decide what use you expect people to make of your music after they have downloaded it.

In other words, if you expect them to play the file again and again – to treat it pretty much as they would a track on a CD, for example – then you'll be looking for something that will offer high quality reproduction, and will inevitably take a long time to download. In this case you'll probably thinking of MP3.

If, on the other hand, you simply want them to get a good enough idea of what your music sounds like – so that they might then do something after they've listened to it (book you for a gig or buy your CD, for example) – then you can go for something cheap and cheerful that will download much more quickly, and might very well stream.

Let's look at the alternatives that are available. To help you get a sense of the varying compression rates that each of the formats offers I've encoded one of my own album tracks – as an MP3 file, a RealAudio file and a Quicktime Movie. The track lasts four minutes and two seconds (short by my standards) and, as an uncompressed .WAV file weighed in at 40.9 Mb. The chances of anyone waiting the hour and a half (and then some!) that this would take to download over the Internet are so remote as to be nonexistent!

Pick of the bunch

MP3

This, of course, is the one that's in the news, and deservedly so. MP3 encoding enables sound files to be heavily compressed – to about a tenth of their original size – and yet offers a level of fidelity which is very close to CD quality. My album track dropped to just 3.7 Mb in this format – saved in the most popular MP3 format of 128kbps at 44kHz. (Don't worry, this will seem quite straightforward once you start playing with an encoder.) This is a huge reduction over the original .WAV file but it would still take a good 10 minutes to download on a 56k modem. This is a reasonable amount of time to wait for something you want, but not many casual visitors are going to want to wait that long unless they already know what they're waiting for. By the way, MP3 can be made to stream, but this isn't its strength. Its real value is as a download and play system, for which it is currently second to none.

INFO

*M*P3 encoding enables sound files to be compressed to about a tenth of their original size.

RealAudio

This is the process that I've been using for a number of years, and it's streaming technology at its very best. Converting my album track to a mono RealAudio format resulted in a file of just 632K. The sound quality is not the best in the world – certainly not as good as MP3 – but the fact that streaming technology allows the site visitor to start listening to the music within a few seconds of clicking on the link is a major consideration. There are an awful lot of people out there who've already got the RealAudio player installed on their machines – something like 150 million of them, apparently, and this format gives them a good enough idea of what I sound like. Because the files load as they're playing, I can provide much longer sound clips than would otherwise be practicable. It's worth bearing in mind, however, that not every ISP will support RealAudio streaming, so it's worth checking that yours will before you go too far down this road.

Quicktime

RealAudio and MP3 are cross platform formats, as at home on a Mac as they are on a PC, but Quicktime has always been most closely associated with the Mac, coming as it does as part of the computer's operating system. However, it is a cross platform application and with the introduction of Quicktime 4 Apple is now making aggressive inroads into the market. With the QDesign Music 2 Codec coming as part of the Quicktime Pro package, it is now fast becoming a serious contender.

Quicktime comes ready installed as part of every Mac's operating system, and with increasing numbers of PC users installing it onto their machines, it's inevitably going to become an attractive proposition. My album track encoded as a Quicktime Movie weighed in at 762K as a stereo 44.1kHz file. As you might expect, it offered better quality than the RealAudio file but not as good as the MP3 – though I have to say it gave it a pretty good run for its money. It's also possible to further compress a Quicktime file so that streaming become an option. By the way, Quicktime is most commonly associated with movies but don't let that bother you – the application will certainly handle moving images, but it's equally happy with just sound.

In the Summer of 2000 Steve Jobs, CEO of Apple, revealed that Apple had logged 36 million downloads of the Quicktime system. Taking this into account along with the fact that Quicktime comes preinstalled on all Macs and some PCs, it's estimated that there are some 50 million people out there with the Quicktime player on their computer. Clearly this is too many people to ignore!

That's the big three then. There are, of course, many other compression systems available but none, at the moment, is quite so popular. There's nothing stopping you experimenting with some of the others, of course, but if you ignore the ones we've looked at you could find that not quite so many people take the opportunity to listen to your music.

Players and encoders

In each of the cases we've looked at the application needed to play the audio file is available as a free download. When It comes to encoding your file into the relevant format, however, you're more likely to find yourself having to put your hand into your pocket.

MP3 players are widely available on the internet but as far as MP3 encoders are concerned the situation is rather more complex. Fraunhofer/Thomson Multimedia, who own the rights to the MP3 technology, appear to be enforcing those rights, and are demanding licence fees from anyone who creates an MP3 encoder. As a result, pretty much all of the freeware encoders which were once so freely available on the web seem to have vanished from sight. This situation may well change at some time in the future and there are certainly a number of "try before you buy" offers from commercial encoders, but it looks likely that if you want to get into MP3 encoding on a regular basis then sooner or later you'll need to put your hand into your pocket for the privilege.

As I've said, MP3 players are legion, but you can find some of the more popular ones at:

SoundJam MP Free2.1 for Mac at http://www.casadyg.com
MacAmp for Mac at http://www.macamp.com
Winamp for PC at http://www.winamp.com/
XAudio Player for all platforms at http://www.xaudio.com/applications/

As far as encoders are concerned you might like to try

Audio Catalyst (PC) at http://www.xingtech.com/mp3/audiocatalyst
SoundJam for Mac at http://www.casadyg.com
QDesign's MVP Player – http://www.mvpsite.com (this will convert CD tracks into MP3 files or to the company's own .mvp format)

And for Mac users with system 9.04 or better the really good news is iTunes, a brilliant piece of software which converts CD tracks to MP3 format and is available as a free download from http://www.apple.com/.

The good news about the RealAudio system is that it is free – both the player and the encoder. There is a "bells and whistles" version available of both applications but I've always been happy enough with the plain vanilla version which you can find at:

http://www.real.com/

The encoder, called the RealProducer is also available from there.

You might need to do a bit of searching about on their site for the free versions of the player and producer, but they are there!

Both are available in Mac and PC versions. Other platforms are supported by earlier versions of the player and encoder at:

http://www.real.com/

The situation with Quicktime is much the same as with MP3 – the player is free but if you want to be able to encode you have to pay – $29.99, to be precise. What you pay for in this case is a registration number since the Quicktime player is actually a fully functioning encoder – but with those functions disabled until registration takes place. Even if you weren't going to be doing that much encoding this could still be a wise investment since registration also gives greater functionality to the player part of the program. (The Quicktime player, by the way, will also play MP3 files, though it doesn't have the "playlist" facilities that many dedicated MP3 players have, so iTunes might be your best bet for that if you're a Mac user.)

Quicktime is available from Apple at:

http://www.apple.com/quicktime/

Preparing for encoding

Before you can begin to encode your music you first need to get it into your computer. Quite how you do this will depend on the encoding system you choose, and on the kind of clip you intend to encode. If you already have your music recorded on a CD, for example, and you wish to encode entire album tracks, then you'll find that both Quicktime and most MP3 encoders – will enable you to encode – or "rip" entire tracks straight from the CD.

If you want to encode segments of tracks then things become just a little more complicated since you'll almost certainly want to introduce fades into the start and end of each clip, and this will involve the use of some sort of sound editing programme. As long as you have audio inputs on your computer – or a sound card similarly equipped – then you're going to have very little difficulty. There is a plethora of software available that will read the data coming from the inputs, save it as a sound file, and allow you to introduce fades as well as edit it in a number of other ways. I generally use SoundEdit 16 for this task, which is a commercial product, but there are a number of shareware products available:

CoolEdit for PC at http://syntrillium.com
Goldwave for PC at http://goldwave.com
Soundhack for Mac at http://hitsquad.com/smm/programs/SoundHack
Sound Studio for Mac at http://www.felttip.com/products/soundstudio

It's important to remember that no encoding system will improve the sound of your music. As we have already seen compression systems always involve the loss of at least some data, and this means that you really want to start with a file that sounds as good as it possibly can do.

INFO

*Y*ou're unlikely to find
  that music which
has been fed to the
inputs from a cassette
tape is ever going to
sound as good as
something that's been
taken straight from a
CD.

This means that you're unlikely to find that music which has been fed to the inputs from a cassette tape is ever going to sound as good as something that's been taken straight from a CD. So, if your music is on a CD, and your sound editing software will read it in this form, that's the route to take – if you can avoid using the analogue inputs on your computer, it's best to do so. If you can't avoid it then just make sure that your tape heads are clean and you use the very best recording that you've got!

By the way, the "ripping" systems that we looked at earlier provide a much better sounding file than does connecting a CD player to a computer's audio inputs. In this latter case the CD player would have to convert the digital data on the CD into analogue data which would then be read by the computer and then converted back into digital, with an inevitable loss of quality. The big advantage of ripping a file is that it stays in a digital format throughout the process.

Though every system has its own requirements there are a number of commonalities. These are the steps you're likely to need to go through, regardless of the file format you're aiming to create.

Getting your sound into the computer, either direct from a CD into the encoder.

Figure 8.2 Ripping a CD track with SoundJam

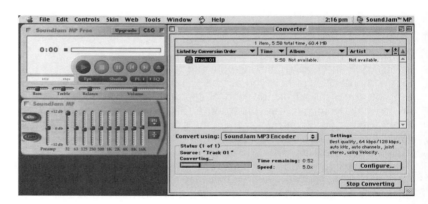

or via a Sound editing program

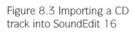

Figure 8.3 Importing a CD track into SoundEdit 16

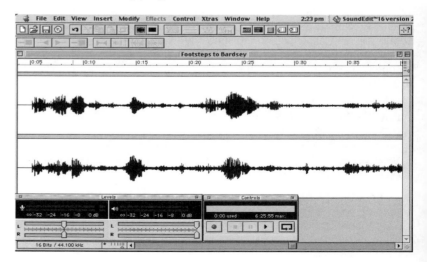

where you might choose to covert the file to mono – it will be smaller if you do, which might well be a consideration, particularly if you're thinking of streaming.

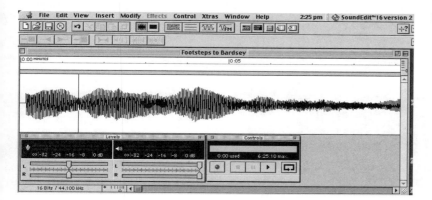

Figure 8.4 A mono file

and where you might choose to introduce fades to the top and tail of your file, thus giving a more professional feel to your work.

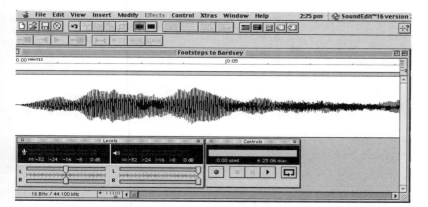

Figure 8.5 Fade in

Having done this you simply need to save the file in a format that your encoder will be able to read. Generally .AIFF or .WAV will be fine.

So much for the generalities – now we need to be more specific.

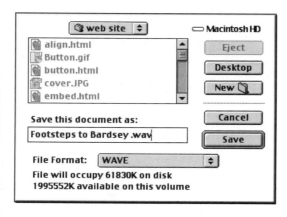

Figure 8.6 Saved as a .WAV file

Encoding for MP3

No two MP3 encoders look the same, but under the skin they all work in much the same way. First you have to identify the file to be encoded – either by locating the file you've just saved onto your computer, or on a CD in your computers CD Rom drive, then you have to configure the settings page. The choices you make here will determine the ultimate file size but, given that most MP3 files on the Internet are encoded at 128kbps at 44kHz that seems like a good choice.

Figure 8.7 The MVP MP3 encoder – and SoundJam's

Because MP3 is primarily a "download and play" system we're going for a stereo file here because that will show the music off at its best. You'll notice that there's a choice here between "sstereo" and "joint stereo". "Joint stereo" introduces a further piece of encoding which essentially encodes the differences between two stereo tracks and thus makes for a slightly smaller file size. Inevitably there's a slight trade off in the quality of the finished file – if in doubt encode it both ways and then decide how much of a difference you think it makes. If you can't tell any difference – or it's so small as to make no difference – then pick the smaller file. Once you've configured the settings there's nothing left for you to do but click the "encode" or "convert" button and wait for the software to do it's job.

Figure 8.8 Encoding

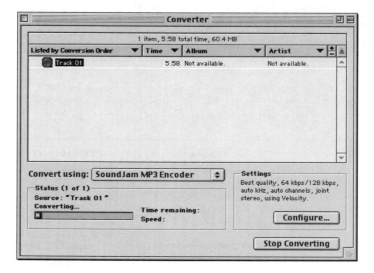

Once the file has been encoded you'll need to play it through on an MP3 player to ensure that you're happy with the results – if you are, then save it until you're ready to put the file onto your web site.

Encoding for RealAudio

Though RealAudio have provided one or two plug-ins which make it possible to export a RealAudio file direct from a sound editing programme the most straightforward way of creating such a file is via RealProducer. So, boot it up and off we go.

Figure 8.9 Choices

You'll be offered a choice of "Recording Assistants". One of these will help you convert an existing file, another will enable you to capture a live sound source, while another one allows you to prepare a file for a live broadcast. Almost certainly you're going to want to convert an existing file. RealAudio doesn't allow you to rip direct from a CD so, ideally, you will already have prepared a file in a sound editing programme.

You then need to steer the program to the file you wish to encode by clicking on that "browse" button.

Figure 8.10 Entering the details

You're then presented with a number of options concerning the description of your work. Some of these will be displayed by the RealPlayer while it is playing your music, and some of them may be used to aid search engines on the web.

The next choice you're confronted with is between SureStream or Single Rate encoding – SureStream will only work in conjunction with the RealServer G2 software, so unless your ISP offers this, you must choose the latter.

Figure 8.11 Unless your files will be streaming from Surestream G2 server, Single Rate should be your choice.

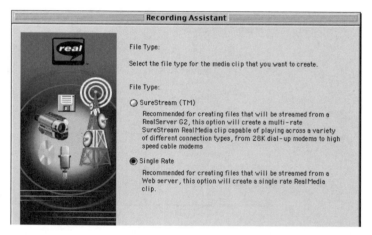

Next you need to decide on how fast a modem will be needed to stream your files. You'll notice that the Recording Assistant talks in terms of selecting 'one or more' target audiences, but this is another option that's available only with SureStream encoding. What you choose here is something of a moot point. No-one is manufacturing 28K modems anymore but there are still quite a few people out there using them. Picking this rate will inevitably give you the worst sound quality of the bunch but you can be sure that just about everyone who tries to listen to your music will be able to do so. 56K will give you a better quality sound, but because there's more data to stream not everybody will be able to hear it without breaks.

Figure 8.12 Selecting the minimum modem speed you want to cater for.

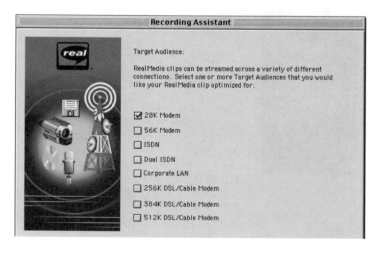

There's nothing stopping you producing two (or more) files for the same piece of music – 28K, 56K and ISDN, for example – but if you think your music sounds "good enough" at 28K then it would be foolish to ignore it,

Different kinds of sound files benefit from slightly different forms of compression, and the next choice you're presented with is to decide what kind of compression your file needs. As you can see from Figure 8.13 this is made painfully easy for you. Almost certainly you'll select 'Music'. I wouldn't dream of using 'Stereo Music' unless you have a target audience of ISDN users!

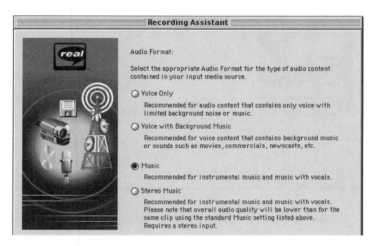

Figure 8.13 File type

When you're asked to indicate where you want the encoded file saved, this is also the time to edit out any spaces in the file name – some servers don't like them, so it's safest to replace them with an underscore.

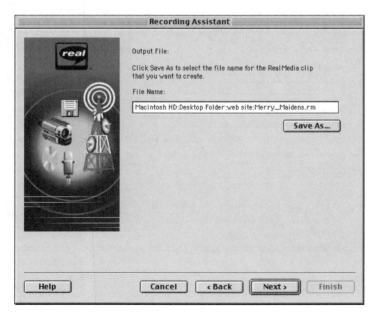

Figure 8.14 Saving your file – no spaces in the filename please

You are given a final chance to amend the information you entered earlier. Once you click 'finish' you'll be on the main encoding window

Figure 8.15 Summary

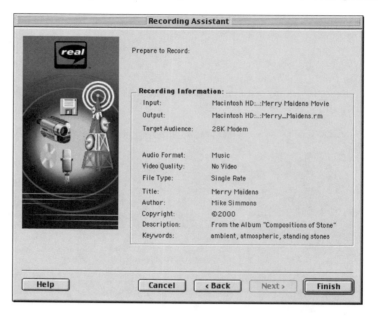

Assuming that you're happy with what you see this is the time to press that 'Start' button and encode your file. If you then wish to look at the encoding statistics you're given the option to do so.

Figure 8.16 Ready to encode

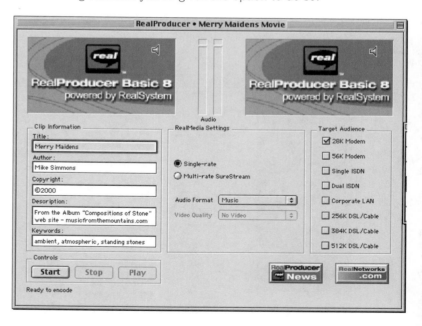

Once you've encoded your file you'll want to listen to it. Click the play button and RealPlayer will boot up, ready loaded with your file.

Figure 8.17 Encoded and ready to play

Of course it doesn't sound as good as it did before you encoded it. You're unlikely to be fooled into thinking that you're listening to a CD – but is it good enough to give someone a fair idea of what your music sounds like? In my case I'd say yes. Certainly the people who buy from my site seem to think it gives them a good enough sense of my music to place an order. Various transients seem to creep in from time to time, there's not the full frequency range that we might like but, given that most people will be listening to it through computer speakers, I'd say that the RealAudio system is very well up to the job.

Incidentally, when you boot the encoder up for the first time you'll notice that you're given the choice of allowing your site visitors the option of saving your RealAudio files onto their hard drive. This is so that they can play them again at a later date without revisiting your site. Whether you permit this or not is up to you, but it's probably a safe enough option to take. Though the encoded files are good, I wouldn't say that they were so good that they were going to do much too damage to your album sales!

Encoding for Quicktime

To reiterate a point I made earlier, if you want to encode for Quicktime you must have the "Pro" version since otherwise you'll find that you don't have the required "Export" or "Save" facilities.

So, boot up Quicktime player and, going to the "File" option in the menu, select "Open Movie" and then steer your way to your sound file. If it's a file you've already prepared and saved as a .WAV you can open it directly into the player. If it's a track on a CD the player will ask you where you want to save it – you have to do this before the file will load into the player.

Figure 8.18 Saving the file

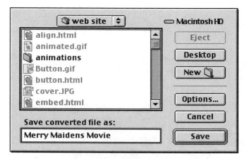

Save your file and then play it through just to make sure you're happy with everything, and then go to "File" and "Export"

You'll want to select "Movie to Quicktime Movie" but we don't need to worry about the "Use" option because we'll go straight to "Options".

Figure 8.19 Exporting

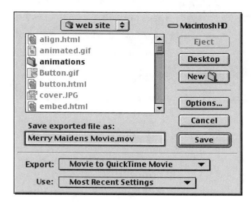

For most of us Quicktime is first and foremost a method of presenting movies rather than sound files and, as you can see, there are two sets of options, one for movies and one for sound. Make sure that "Movies" and "Prepare for Internet Streaming" are unchecked, and that "Sound" is checked, and then click on "settings" for sound.

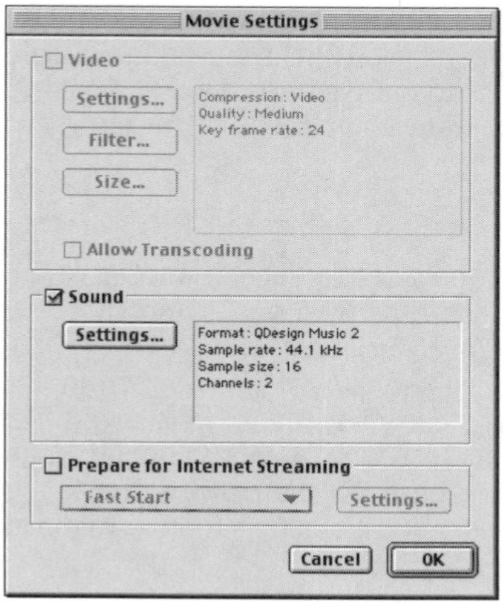

Figure 8.20 Settings

This is where you'll select the compressor for your file and the best one for a music file is QDesign Music 2, so that's the one to select. Because we want to produce a high quality file we'll select 16 bit stereo at 44.1 kHz. Having made that choice click on OK, and again on the previous menu as it appears, and finally click "Save". What you'll discover now is that though the QDesign Music 2 is a very impressive compression system it's not the fastest in the world, so you've probably got time to make yourself a quick cup of tea while it gets on with its job! To be honest you've probably got time for some cheese on toast too, and a second cup of tea ...

Figure 8.21 choosing a compressor

Once your file has been compressed open it up in the player because we've got just a little more to do. (Make sure that it is your new file that you open up, by the way, and not the .AIFF or .WAV file that you had prior to compression. You're looking for the one with a .MOV extender.

Figure 8.22 Compressed and ready to play

Now, once you're played the file through to check that everything is OK go to "Get Info" from the "Movie" menu.

Select "Movie" (not "Soundtrack") in the left hand options box and "Annotations" in the one on the right.

Figure 8.23 Click "Add" for annotations

The Quicktime Player has an "Information" tray which displays any information that has been embedded in a file, Figure 8.24.

To embed just such information, click on the "Add" button and you'll
see a range of fields – everything from "Album" to "Writer" – into which
information can be added. There's a few points to look out for here,
however.

Any alpha-numeric information can be entered into any field – in
other words, you don't have to restrict yourself to putting the album
title in the field marked "Album"

Though all the information you enter will be saved with the file, and
be accessible from the "get info" option in the menu, only the following
fields will appear in the player's Info Tray – Artist, Author, Album,
Comment, Copyright, Director, Description, Full Name, Information,
Performers, Producer and Writer.

A maximum of three of these fields will be displayed in the Info Tray.
And a fairly obvious one this, if you enter more text in a field than can
be displayed – it won't all be displayed!

So, select a field and enter the information you want to enter and
click "Add". Select another field, click "Add" again and so on.

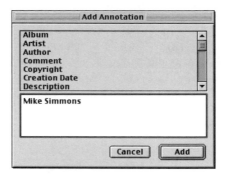

Regardless of what field names you select, the information I'd most
want to appear in the tray is my name, the name of the piece of music,
and my web site address. That way, wherever the file winds up, anyone
wanting to find out more about my music could trace it to its source.
(And offer me a huge record deal, vast sums of money, fast cars, holi-
days in the sun, my own yacht etc etc etc)

Once you've added the information you wish to displayed, close the
info box and click "Save" from the File menu and you're done.

Quicktime streaming

While we were going through the process of creating a Quicktime file
you'll remember that I told you to leave that "Prepare for Internet

Streaming" box unchecked. What's this, you must be thinking – can Quicktime stream? Well, yes it can, in two different formats, in fact. One of these, RTSP streaming, depends on the file being held on a special RTSP server and, given that this is not an option that many ISP's currently provide, I'm not going to go into the relevant details in this book. The other format, HTTP streaming is more of a viable proposition, however, and is well worth looking at.

So, back to "Options" from the Export menu and this time check that "Internet Streaming". You have a choice now between "Hinted Streaming", "Fast Start" and "Fast Start – Compressed Header."

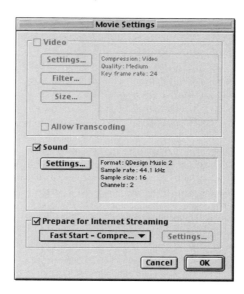

Figure 8.26 Settings for streaming

"Hinted Streaming" is only an option for RTSP streaming, so your real choice is going to be between the other two. "Fast Start – Compressed Header" will give you a file which will load a little more quickly than "Fast Start", but it won't play on old players prior to version 3. Given that at the time of writing Quicktime is now up to version 4, with Version 5 very much on the horizon, it's unlikely that there are going to be too many people using version 2, so it's probably worth taking the risk and going for the compressed header.

While RealAudio makes things easy for you by asking about the modem speed of your target audience, Quicktime leaves you to work things out for yourself. Essentially this means dividing your file size by it's length in seconds and then making a shrewd guess about the likelihood of it getting through an average modem on an average day. So let's think about a two minute clip of music which has been encoded by Quicktime and resulted in a 380Kb File.

380 divided by 120 would give us 3.1Kb

A 28.8K modem is theoretically capable of shifting data at 3.6Kb per second (remember, that 28.8 is kilobits, not bytes) but in practice – clogged Internet, poor phone lines – will always fall short of this. At first glance then it looks like our file is not going to stream very effectively. However, 28.8K is now quite a low modem speed, and if you're prepared to risk some of your site visitors not being able to stream then it looks like our file size should work well enough.

If you do need to make your file smaller you could try reducing the sample rate (though you'd be best to steer clear of 11.127kHz and 22.125 kHz since, though they'll work well enough on Macs they might prove rather more troublesome on PCs) or converting the file from stereo to mono. Inevitably, getting the file size small enough is going to involve you in a little bit of trial and error but it's time well spent. Just one thing to remember while you're doing this – always go back to the source file each time you try a different combinations of settings – don't try to compress an already compressed file since it can lead to unpredictable – and unpleasant – results.

One final point. You may have noticed a whole range of "streaming" settings while we were setting up Quicktime and you may be wondering why I seem to have ignored them. No, I know they're there, but they are only relevant to RTSP streaming, and so not an available choice for the HTTP option.

Getting your file onto your site

So you've encoded your file and you're ready to get it onto your web site. As far as MP3 and Quicktime files are concerned the HTML you'll need is very straightforward, and something like:

```
Here's a <A HREF="filename.mov">track </A>off my new album
```

or

```
Here's a <A HREF="filename.mp3">track </A>off my new album
```

will do fine. It makes sense, though, to warn your visitor about what it is that they're letting themselves in for, so adding the size of the file:

```
Here's a <A HREF="filename.mov">track </A>off my new album
(842K)
```

might be a good deal friendlier!

You will have noticed that the RealAudio file your encoder produced came with a .rm extender. Given the HTML we've already looked at for Quicktime and .MP3 files it would be reasonable to expect that all you'd need for a RealAudio file would be:

```
<A HREF="filename.rm">here's my RealAudio file</A>
```

No such luck, however! This is a mistake that many people make – particularly those who don't bother to read the Read Me files. This piece of

HTML works fine while the site is sitting on your own hard drive but, once it's been beamed up to your server what you actually need is this:

```
<A HREF="filename.ram">here's my RealAudio file</A>
```

Meta files

So what's happening here? Your actual sound file is called "music.rm", for example, but you have to create another file – which will be called "music.ram" in order for the music to stream. This file is called a "meta file" and simply directs the browser to the sound file by indicating its path – and its this meta file that you link to.

If you choose to use the "publish" option that the RealAudio encoder provides then you'll find that this meta file is created automatically for you, but there are disadvantages in taking this option in that the layout of the page is dictated by RealAudio and though you can edit the page, you need to take a good deal of care while you're doing so. Given it's so easy to create your own meta file you might prefer to do it yourself.

All you need to do is boot up your text editor and key in the exact path to the RM file on your server – in my case it might be something like:

```
http://www.musicmtn.demon.co.uk/sounds/stone.rm
```

and then save your work as a text file with the .ram extender. The meta file for my "stone.rm" file would, in this case, be called "stone.ram" and the HTML from my web page would be

```
<A HREF="stone.ram">here's a track from my album "Compositions of Stone"</A>
```

This is so important that It really feels worth repeating myself. I want to stress that the meta file consists of nothing but the path – it contains no HTML at all. It's just a text file. If you do decide to create your own meta files, it might be worth contacting your ISP before getting too involved in the process. The ISP I use (Demon) will automatically generate an RAM file the moment an RM file is placed on its server, which certainly saves me from a fair bit of angst!

If you turn back to RealProducer, you'll notice that amongst the tools on the final encoding page there is also the option to "Create Web Page". If you click on this, you'll find another assistant that will help write the HTML for your page and create that meta file for you. Inevitably, as you can see from Figure 8.27, there's a pretty strong RealAudio presence to pages created in this way.

One thing to be aware of. however. If you choose the "Create Web Page" option there is an assumption that you will also be using the "Publish Web Page" tool that is also provided. If you don't do this then you'll find that the meta file won't work once you beam it to the server. The publish option automatically updates the file as it's transmitted.

Personally, I wouldn't worry too much about either of these two features. Creating your own meta file isn't much of a problem and you'll

Figure 8.27 A RealProducer
designed page

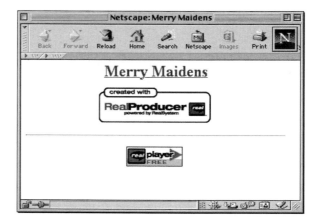

have far more freedom in designing your own page rather than letting RealAudio do it for you.

MIDI

One music system that we haven't looked at yet, and one which obviates all the difficulties involved in compressing vast sound files, is the one that is likely to be most familiar to many readers of this book – MIDI. As I'm sure you know, MIDI files are very small, since they contain a set of instructions about a piece of music, rather than the sound itself. It's perfectly possible to call up a MIDI file on your site with nothing more complicated than a tag like:

```
<A HREF="filename.mid">here's a MIDI file for you to play</A>
```

The difficulty here, however, is that you have no way of knowing what the end user will be playing that MIDI file with. Almost certainly, Mac users will hear it on the built-in Quicktime Musical Instrument Set, while PC users will probably play it back on whatever soundcard they have installed, if any. Paradoxically, therefore, it is those who are most able to introduce MIDI onto their web sites who are likely to be most reluctant to do so. When I'm writing music I spend a lot of time – as any MIDI musician does – auditioning synths and samplers to determine exactly the right sound for the piece I'm working on. To then have the music reduced down to a PC General MIDI set of unpredictable quality is not an attractive proposition. I'm not denying that MIDI has its place – but that place could be on pretty much any site other than one showcasing a MIDI musician's work!

Embedding files

You don't have to link a file with the <A HREF> tag, by the way. There is an alternative which offers a more elegant appearance, though it's not without it's difficulties. Just try this

```
<EMBED SRC="filename.mov" CONTROLLER=TRUE
AUTOSTART=TRUE LOOP=TRUE > </EMBED>
```

and see what happens when you open it up in your browser – you don't have to use a .mov file, by the way – the command works equally well with .MIDI or .WAV files.

If you're using a fairly recent version of Netscape or Internet Explorer you should see a small control panel appear on your page while the music starts to play automatically.

Figure 8.28 An embedded file

If you're using an older version of Internet Explorer you may find that nothing happens at all, because the <EMBED> tag was introduced by Netscape and is not, strictly speaking, pure HTML. If you don't include that "CONTROLLER = TRUE" tag you may find, depending on the age of your browser, that the music plays but there's no way or stopping it. With LOOP switched to TRUE this means that you'll probably find you lose some visitors to your site who simply can't bear to listen to the music any longer!

The great advantage of the <EMBED> tag is that, unlike the <A HREF> tag, your site visitor won't find themselves jumping to another page – or a helper appliction – when they click on the link. The great disadvantage is that though the <EMBED> tag gives a more attractive appearance to your page this will be of little comfort to the visitor with an older version of Internet Explorer who won't even realise that there is some music that they should be listening to!

By all means feel free to experiement with this tag, but just bear in mind that it has its limitations. If you decide that the best course of action for your site is to provide RealAudio streaming and MP3 or Quicktime "download and play" then you may wonder whether you really need worry about <EMBED>ding your sound anyway!

Video

If you've been working with RealAudio or Quicktime you will have noticed that you could also be producing your own video files. It's an interesting thought – if people are going to enjoy listening to your music, how much more might they enjoy watching you at the same time? As ever, it all comes down to bandwidth because, inevitably, video files are even bigger than sound files. Having said that – if you're tempted, why not give it a try?

Figure 8.29 Sound *and* vision

Again, a streaming file will need to be much more heavily compressed than would a "download and play" file, so it really makes sense to start with as high a file quality as you can get – digital is by far the best choice if you can use it. Of course you'll need video inputs on your computer if your going to choose this option. and the appropriate software but these are by no means as rare as they were just a few years ago.

The HTML is the same as for an audio file, so in the case of Quicktime all you'd need would be:

Here's a <A HREF="filename.MOV">movie </A>of our last gig

One final point – don't make video the only way that anyone can get to listen to your music – or see what you or your band look like. Most visitors are probably not going to bother to wait for a video file to download, so make sure that you provide a picture and sound file too!

Publish and be damned! 9

If you've been following this book through page by page you've probably got a site by now that's well worth getting onto the Internet. How you do this will depend more than anything else on your ISP but there are a number of commonalities worth going through.

The process of "publishing" a web site involves copying the files that you have created on your hard drive onto your ISP's server. They will provide you with an address for this, so that you know where to put it, and they'll provide you with a password – or ask you to give them one – so that they know it's you putting it there.

There are a number of different pieces of software able to perform this task and you may find your ISP supplies you with one in some sort of support package, but the important thing to bear in mind is that the relationship between all the files that you put on the server must stay exactly the same as it was on your hard drive. In other words, you need to copy all the directories and folders as well as the actual files and you need to make sure that those files end up in the correct folders.

Some pieces of software will beam up your entire site to the server in one go, so there's no risk of any such difficulties, but if your's doesn't, it's worth taking care, or you'll find yourself confronted by broken link icons.

Two popular pieces of publishing software are Fetch (Mac) and Cute (PC). Both can be downloaded from the internet from any of the many shareware sites such as:

http://shareware.cnet.com/
http://www.websitecentral.co.uk/
http://download.cnet.com/
http://davecentral.com/
http://pure-mac.com/

though Fetch is also directly available from:

http://fetchsoftworks.com

Figure 9.1 Working with Fetch

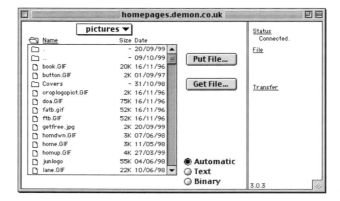

Both present you with a visual directory of all your files on the ISP's server and allow you to upload, move, delete, and replace files. I particularly like Cute because of the way in which it presents you with two directories – one showing the site on your hard drive the other the site on the server.

Figure 9.2 ... and working with Cute

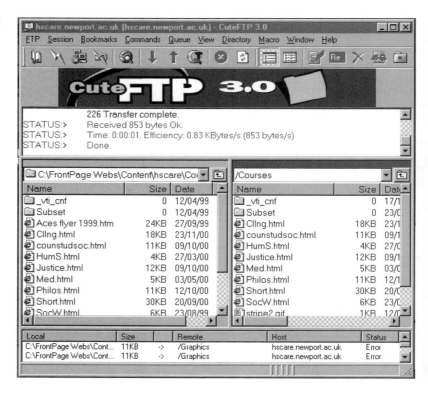

Once your site is on the server it should be visible to the world at large within 24 hours or so, often much sooner, but don't panic if it's not immediately available – different ISPs handle uploads in different ways. Once the site is up and running this is not the time to delete all those files currently located on your hard drive. These are the files that you will be working on whenever you want to make a change to your site, remember, so they are a vital part of your system. Whenever you edit a page just beam it up to your ISP's server and it will replace the page of the same name that's already on the server.

Better mousetrap

Having created the perfect web site it would be fair to imagine that you've got nothing more to do but sit back and wait for people to visit it. Sadly this is not the case. The world is full of people who have built a better mousetrap and are still waiting for someone to beat a path to their door, and given the fact that there are millions of sites out there you're still going to have to do some more work if you want people to visit yours.

The most obvious way of getting people to visit you is to tell them what your address is! I try to make mine pretty ubiquitous: I put it on all my album covers, and I put it on the signature of my emails. It's also on my letter heading and my invoices. I also swap links with other people from time to time but, as I've already explained, I do try to ensure that there's some kind of relevance in making that swap. It can sometimes be a temptation to swap with just anyone, and as a result the Internet is swamped with vast lists of links which have very little coherence or logic to them. My suspicion is that these are the lists that nobody reads and the links that nobody follows ...

Register your site

The most important thing to do, however, is to register your site with a search engine or, to be more precise, with each and every search engine that you can possibly find. Search engines are, essentially, vast databases. When you enter a word or phrase into the space provided, the engine searches the database and comes up with pages that give a good match to the data you entered. Given that most people have a favourite engine, and that many of the new visitors to any site arrive as a result of carrying out a search, it makes sense to spread the word about your site as far and wide as you possibly can.

Most search engines have programs called 'spiders' which constantly trawl the web, following links and updating their databases accordingly. If a spider finds your site, therefore, it will be added to that search engine's database. However, this will only happen if it is able to follow a link to your site from another. As a consequence, if your site is new it may be a long time before this happens – and it won't happen at all if no-one else has a link to your site. You can speed the process up somewhat by letting the search engines know of your presence yourself. If you go to any search engine you'll generally find a link somewhere named something like "add URL" or "add your site" (Figure 9.3).

Fairly obviously, this is the link you should click on and, having done so, you'll be talked through the process of adding your site to their database.

Some engines will simply ask you for your URL while others will ask you to give them a few key words to describe your site and, perhaps, a brief overall description. Brief generally means 20 words or so, and if you decide to ignore this restriction you'll simply find that your major essay will be cut off in it's prime after – you've guessed it – 20 words.

Figure 9.3 Submitting your site

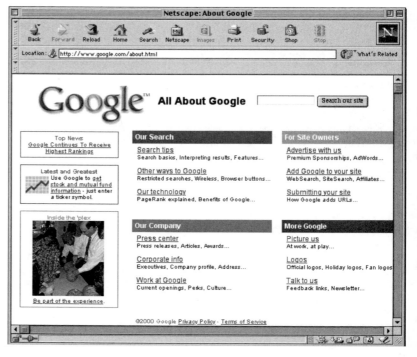

Make the 20 words count, and make sure that the key words you use are the kind of thing that people might enter into a search engine if they were looking for a site like yours.

Figure 9.4 Adding details

Figure 9.5 A short cut

It's while going through the process of adding your site details to the search engines that you realise just how many of the things there are out there but, at least to some extent, help is at hand.

There are a number of facilities on the web that will submit your site to a large number of engines. Very often they will operate a kind of two-tier process where they will submit your site to a small number of engines for free, or a large number for a fee. A couple of such sites that you might like to try are -

http://www.search-engine-index.co.uk/Submit/
http://www.hammonds.freeserve.co.uk/submit.htm

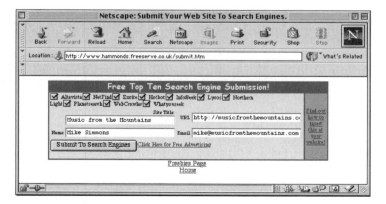

Figure 9.6 ...and another one

But there are literally hundreds of them out there – just try a search with something like "submit+site" and you'll see what I mean. Once you've submitted your site you'll generally receive a torrent of emails from the various search engines telling you that your site has been registered and/or will be visited (by a 'spider') in the next few days.

META tags

You can, if you want to, leave it at that, but if you take a little more time, you can influence the way in which your final entry will appear to anyone doing a search. You might remember that way back at the beginning of this book we brushed past META tags, and I promised that we'd come back to them some time in the future. This is that time. META tags sit between the <HEAD> and </HEAD> tags, and provide a wide range of information which a spider can use to categorise your site. The two most important META tags are 'description' and 'keywords'. If I show you how I've used them you'll get the idea of how they work. Here's the description from my site:

```
<META NAME="description" CONTENT="My name is Mike Simmons. I write music to dream to – atmospheric music weaving layers of natural and artificial sound..">
```

You can do exactly the same on your site, replacing all the text within the second pair of quotation marks with your own description.

My keywords tag, which takes a similar form, is as follows:

```
<META NAME="keywords" CONTENT="New Age Music, Relaxing, Meditation, Ambient, Portmeirion, Aberdaron, Anelog, Bardsey Island, Music from the Mountains">
```

FANTASY TIME

I must own up to harbouring a fantasy that one day Stephen Spielberg will stumble across my site, love my music, and ask if he can use some of it in his next film. Just a little unlikely, you might think, but a lot more likely than the chance of him breaking into my studio, pausing to listen to a couple of tracks, and then asking if he can use some of it.

In both cases there should be no carriage returns, just one long string of lower case text which is presented as one line. If you visit someone else's site and view the HTML there as source you'll see the way in which other people are using META tags to increase the chances of effective indexing of their sites.

You can have as many keywords as you like, in fact, and it really is a case of the more the merrier. I've only included a few from my own site to save you from terminal boredom, but it's important to bear in mind that the spiders that visit your site are not particularly bright. I know that Portmeirion and Aberdaron etc are all in Gwynedd, for example, but the spider won't, and when it visits my site it will only index it as relating to Gwynedd if I put "Gwynedd" amongst those key words. If I don't include "Gwynedd" then anyone entering that word into a search engine won't find my site coming up, and so they won't pay me a visit.

Spiders aren't bright but nor are they totally stupid, by the way, and the days when you could repeat every word several times just to get a higher rating in the search engines are long gone. I tend to think of META tags as being something like bait for a fish – the more effective they are the more spiders are likely to be caught – and the more people are likely to visit your site.

Site maintenance

However, you don't just want to attract people to your site, you also want to keep them there for as long as possible once they've arrived. You'll do this by making your site interesting, of course, but also by making sure that it's up to date and not riddled with broken links. Even if no-one else visits your site it's imperative that you do, checking that everything still works and generally looking after it. This is one of the big advantages of creating your own site rather than paying someone else to do it – you can keep it up-to-date.

Broken links

Even if you don't need to change the information on your site that often you still can't simply leave it to look after itself. Because you will have made links to sites other than your own you will need to visit you own site from time to time just to make sure that those links are still working. If you find a broken link you can email the owner of that site to see if they've changed things at their end. If you get no response and know that there was nothing wrong with the link previously your best bet is to delete it from your site. Broken links are a frustration to all who click on them!

You may also get the odd email from someone having difficulty with some part of your site that doesn't make much sense to you. Don't ignore them just because everything looks perfectly fine on your own machine – carefully read what they say and then go back to the HTML code to see if you can identify anything that would cause the fault they describe. If they've gone to the trouble to email you they probably won't mind you getting back to them for some more information. What computer platform are they using? What browser? What version? If one person bothers to contact you it's fair to assume that there are many more who don't, and if you want to attract as many people as possible to your site it's unlikely that you're going to do it with dodgy HTML!

Under construction?

Finally, and a totally personal opinion – resist the temptation to use fancy "under construction" graphics. Pretty much everyone's site is constantly under construction, and no-one wants to wait for a graphic to download – particularly an animated one – to tell them that yours is too!

TIP

If I visit your site in December and find only a gig list for the previous October I'm not likely to be very impressed – but I might well be interested in seeing some pictures that were taken at one of those gigs!

10 Selling on the net

Once you've got your site up and running what you do next will largely depend on what function you hope it will perform. You might have simply wanted to tell the world about yourself and, if you're lucky, drum up a few extra gigs. But what if you've got something to sell?

More and more musicians are producing their own albums and see the Internet is an ideal medium for advertising their products. I'm one of them, and you may well be too – but how is it actually possible to make that sale?

Cheque or credit card?

Let's imagine the person who has stumbled across your home page completely out of the blue. They've liked the feel of your site sufficiently to want to listen to some of your music, and they've liked what they've heard there sufficiently to want to buy the album. So they send you an email to say so – and this is the point at which things can grind to a halt. You've got the album, and they've got the money, and you want to swap. Sending them the album isn't too much of a problem, you just stick it in a Jiffy bag and put it in the post. But what about the money?

If you live in the same country as your customer then they can send you a cheque. This system lacks something in the way of immediacy, of course, but it does work. If they're not in the same country, however, then a cheque is unlikely to be too much use to you because by the time the bank has taken their cut for converting it to your own currency there's not going to be that much left for you. I live in the UK and although that's where most of my sales come from I still get regular orders from the USA. I charge £10.50 for a CD and the bank would charge £6 to convert a dollar cheque into sterling. Clearly this is not a sensible way to do business!

If you've been in business – and trading with a business bank account – for some while then your bank may well let you become a Credit Card merchant. You can then contact one of the Internet e-commerce companies – Worldpay.com and Netbanx.com are two that spring to mind – who will help you with some of the intricacies of selling on the web. Obviously this is going to make it much easier for your customers to "impulse buy" and is generally a much neater solution than worrying about cheques – but it's a solution that comes with a price tag.

The problem is that it's not a cheap business, and the expense involved could very easily eat up the bulk of any profit you're likely to make on sales. The smaller the fish you are, the less useful it will be as an option. If you really think that you'll manage to shift several thousand copies of your album(s) every year then it's going to be worth following up – if you're selling a few hundred then I personally wouldn't worry about it.

Other possibilities

If you don't have a business account, or if you don't feel that your sales are likely to warrant the not inconsiderable costs that being an Internet Credit Card Merchant is likely to cost you, then you're going to need to find some way of coming under the wing of someone who can take payment by credit card or, alternatively, who can offer some other payment method.

One such company is Global Internet Billing. They can be contacted at:

http://www.glintbill.com

and have set up a demo site at

http://www.musicpayment.com/

Global Internet Billing – an option for the small internet trader

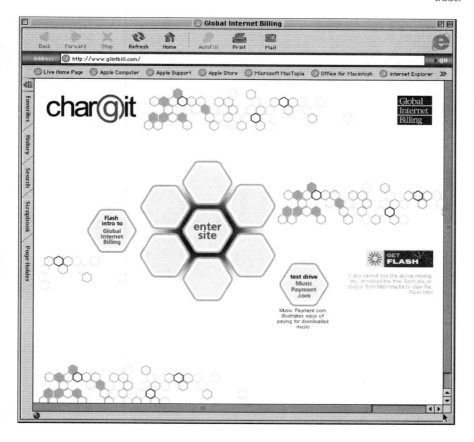

This is a mock-up of an Internet music site and proposes several interesting payment options. One of these is that the actual download connection should be billed, through them, at a premium or international rate. Another is the marketing of scratch cards which would be sold in newsagents much like prepaid mobile phone cards and then used to "buy" the download,

It's difficult to know how soon these systems – or something quite different – will become commonplace, but it seems very likely that a number of "middlemen" will establish themselves over the next few years making it possible for small traders to do business on the Internet.

MP3 sales

There is one other way of selling your music on the web that might be worth considering, and that's by getting your music onto one of the sites dedicated to distributing MP3 files. Perhaps the largest such site in the UK is Peoplesound, but there are very many others, including the massive MP3.com in the States, who carry literally thousands of such files.

The routine with each of these companies varies, but there are many similarities. Generally you'll be offered a page of your own on their site, and you'll be invited to submit a photo, details about you or your band, and one or more MP3 files.

Peoplesound
Peoplesound have a policy of auditioning the music they put on their site so your first step would be to download a signup pack from them on

http://www.peoplesound.com/artists/signup/signnew.htm

Figure 10.1 Peoplesound wll set up a web page for your album if they like your music

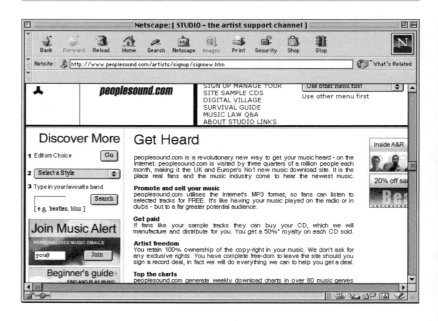

This is available as either a Word Document or an Acrobat File and once you've read that your next task is to fill in the paperwork and send them a copy of your album. They expect you to identify at least two tracks from the album that you will allow them to make available for free download and, if they like what they hear – and they like about 80% of the music sent to them – they'll set up a web page for your album. People who like what they hear when they listen to those free downloads are able to buy copies of the album – which Peoplesound burn to order from your original copy – and the profit on the deal is split between you and the company.

There was a time when Peoplesound also offered a £100 advance for each new act that they signed (I was one of the lucky ones) but this has now been phased out.

The important thing to remember, though – advance or no advance – is that what they are offering is a non-exclusive distribution deal. In other words, they will attempt to sell your music for you but don't mind other people doing the same thing. So, if you suddenly become a mega-star and find executives from Sony constantly hanging around your house trying to sign you up you're free to do so – because either party in your deal with Peoplesound can terminate the deal whenever they wish to.

MP3.com

MP3.com have a slightly different arrangement in that they accept everything that's sent to them. You can find them on:

http://www.mp3.com/

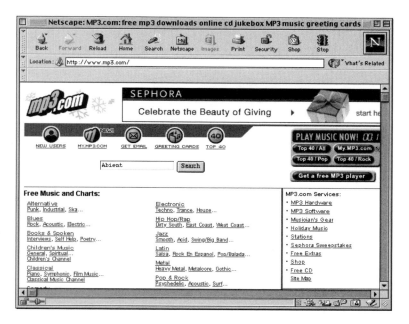

Figure 10.2 MP3.com accept everything that's sent to them

from where you'll need to steer yourself towards "newartist signup"

MP3.com ask you to provide an artist or band name (seems reasonable!), an email address and a postal address. They also invite you to provide an MP3 file and one or two pictures.

It's probably better not to get too excited about the possibilty of making untold riches from any of these sites but, given that they all seem to offer non-exclusive deals it's hard to see what you've got to lose.

And finally

Domain names

You may have seen adverts in the computer press for Domain Names and be wondering what that's all about. After all, you got a domain name when you first signed up with your ISP, so why should you want another one?

Well, you got a name all right, but it probably doesn't sound as professional as it could do. When I started this book my site address was http://www.musicmtn.demon.co.uk. There's nothing wrong with it as an address, but it hardly slips off the tongue and I've lost count of the number of times I've had to spell out that "musicmtn"

By registering a domain name with one of the companies offering this service I can choose pretty much any name I want – assuming someone else hasn't already got it – and pick something that makes immediate sense – and is a good deal easier to dictate over the phone.

As you will already have realised, the name I chose was:

musicfromthemountains.com

It was an incredibly simple process and involved very little more than filling in some forms on the Internet and handing over some cash – or, at least, giving a credit card number.

I didn't have to change my ISP since anyone typing the new domain name into their browser will be routed directly to my existing site by the company offering the service. The beauty of this arrangement is that anyone entering the old domain name – which is printed on the back of all my tapes and CDs – will still find themselves at my site because that's the domain name that my ISP actually recognises.

So what did I do? I chose to use a company called "Simplynames", simply because they are local to me and a friend had used them and been happy with their service – but there are many other companies offering something similar.

These are the steps I went through:
I decided I wanted the name to be musicfromthemountains, so first I had to check that no-one else was already using the name (Figure 11.1).

Figure 11.1 Checking a name
for availability

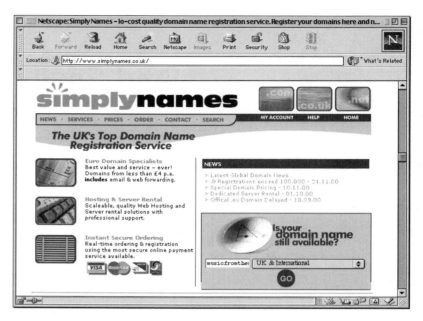

They weren't! I could select from quite a range. You might be wondering about the difference between ".com" and ".co.uk" – there's none at all really, except that ".com " – standing for "commercial" – is somehow seen to be that much more businesslike – so that's the one I went for.

Figure 11.2 Spoilt for choice

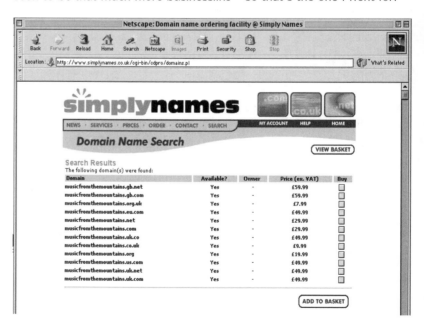

I then had to make my selection, give a range of personal details and select a user name and password for myself. Later in the same day I received an email from the company telling me that the name had been registered. I returned to their site and set up the routing links for my

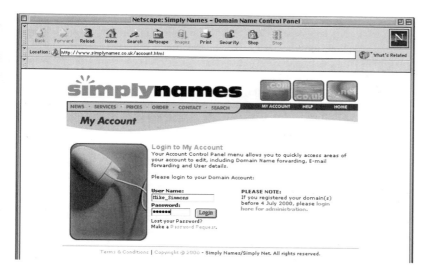

Figure 11.3 Logging in to the account

email and web site – this simply involved filling in a couple of forms saying where I wanted site visitors to be directed when they entered the new address into their browser. Within 24 hours the system was up and working.

Besides looking more businesslike, the other big advantage of having registered the domain name is that it means that if I ever changed my ISP I wouldn't have to change my domain name – I'd simply have to change the links with the company with whom I registered the name.

Is that it, then?

Though by now you know everything you need to know in order to tell the world about your music, as far as HTML is concerned we've barely scratched the surface. The further we venture beneath that surface, however, the more complicated things can become. Just try entering the following piece of code:

```
<MARQUEE>Here is a piece of scrolling text which will scroll, reasonably enough, across your screen </MARQUEE>
```

and now try opening it – and this is important – in Internet Explorer. There are a number of subsidiary tags related to the <MARQUEE> tag which will give you more control over the way in which the text performs, but you can see from this small example that this could be quite a useful effect.

Now try opening the same piece of code in Netscape and you'll simply see a piece of static text. Very dull – so what's going on here? HTML is, essentially, a live language, and like any language it has been subject to change and development. A few years ago, simply getting pictures onto a web site was considered to be pretty impressive, but now we have the potential for sound, video, animations and so on. Inevitably, a great deal of the impetus for these innovations has come from the major players in the browser market, each of whom is striving to produce the dominant product.

There is a body called the World Wide Web Consortium which attempts to standardise HTML, and from time to time 'suggests' what version of HTML we should be using, but inevitably this is something of an uphill struggle in the context of the scramble between Netscape and Microsoft to produce the industry standard browser. Thus, the Consortium 'suggests' that HTML 4 should be the adopted standard, but neither of the big two support all the features described in that version – and both of them have introduced innovations of their own which are not part of the specification, and which are not supported by their rival.

Thus, Internet Explorer supports the <MARQUEE> tag, and has done for several years but (quite rightly) ignores the infamous <BLINK> tag. Netscape, on the other hand, is delighted to display <BLINK> text in all its glory but, as we have seen, will have no truck with the <MARQUEE> tag whatsoever. It's always seemed to me hugely impressive that all those synth manufacturers could have sat down together at NAMM in 1982 to agree the MIDI standard. When you consider the difficulty involved in getting just two manufacturers to agree over HTML, it's little short of miraculous!

What all this means in practice is that you have to bear in mind that the more sophisticated your coding becomes the less likely it is that every visitor to your site will be able to enjoy it. Not every feature you include in your web site will necessarily be supported by both the major browsers. Nor will every visitor to your site be using the most up-to-date version of that browser, be it Navigator, Internet Explorer or something completely different! This is not an insurmountable problem, and can largely be overcome by simply being aware of the limitations within which you are working. Unless you are working with a captive audience, all of whom are using the same version of the same browser, you must be aware that what you see on your screen may well not be what other people see on theirs!

So where to from here?

What you do next will be up to you. You may choose to go deeper and deeper into HTML, introducing all the new technologies as they become available.You may choose to keep your site maintained as it is and get back to your music. HTML is frustrating, gratifying and fun. It's also incredibly seductive. It's all too easy to find yourself doing something because it can be done, rather than because it's a good idea to do it. Your site can be whatever you want to make it – you can fill it with animations, flashing words and all manner of bells and whistles, or you can maintain a Zen-like simplicity. Whichever you choose (and I know which one I'd go for!), I hope it helps you to get your music to a wider audience.

INFO

The more sophisticated your coding becomes the less likely it is that every visitor to your site will be able to enjoy it.

Checklist 12

Have you:

- Looked at some other sites to get some idea of what yours might look like?
- Thought through the navigation system - are you going to use frames? .
- If you're going to create your own graphics have you located a graphics program that you feel moderately familiar with?
- If you're going to include photographs on your site have you got access to a scanner?
- Are you going to use an authoring program, or write raw HTML yourself? If the former, have you identified which one you're going to use. (If the latter, have you got a cool head?!)
- Have you got a copy of Internet Explorer and Netscape installed on your machine? You need both to make sure that you're aware of any differences that might crop up when viewing your pages with different browsers.
- If you're a Mac user have you got access to a PC somewhere so that you can check what your work will look like on a different platform? (and if you're a PC user...)
- Have you managed to establish a few interesting links to other sites that your visitors are going to find worth following?
- An interesting one this. Have you thought about getting someone else to test your site for you, just so that you can check whether those discreet little links are a little more discreet than they need to be? (In other words, can they find them?) Have they managed to find their way around without you prompting them?
- Are you going to put sound on your site? If so, have you decided which format(s) you're going to use?
- Have you located the appropriate encoding software?
- Have you got a basic sound editing programme that will let you manipulate sound files before encoding?
- Are you going to sign up with one or two (or more) of the MP3 companies currently operating?
- Have you remembered that just because you've got a super fast ADSL connection not everyone that visits your site will have?
- Have you managed to resist all the bells and whistles you could add

to your site if you wanted to, but that won't really make any difference to your site visitor except that they will make your pages that much slower to download?
- Have you located which ISP you're going to use to host your site?
- Do they support Real Audio streaming?
- Have you decided whether to register a domain name:
  (a) So that you've got a name that's easy to remember and that sounds professional?
  (b) So that if you become dissatisfied with your ISP you can make the switch to a new one without having to get all your publicity material reprinted?
- If your ISP didn't provide you with it, have you got hold of the appropriate software for uploading your pages to the ISP's server?
- Have you tried a few experiments with it, just to make sure you understand the system? (Just upload a page or two and then see if you can view it with a browser pointed at your web site address.)
- Are you going to try selling direct from your site? If so, have you tried exploring the web to see what opportunities are currently available?
- Once your site is up and running, have you tried submitting your site to as many search engines as you can find?
- Have you committed yourself to checking your site on a regular basis, making sure that the material you've got is still relevant and that all the links are still working?
- It's probably time to get back to making some music then!

Two weeks later:
- Have you gone back to your site to make sure that all the links are still working and that everything's still working?

Then:
- It's probably time to get back to making some music then!

And so it goes on!

Frequently asked questions (FAQs)

This book started off in life as a series of articles in the highly esteemed *Sound on Sound* magazine. While the series was running (and for many months afterwards) I received a steady flow of emails from people wanting to know more. Many of those queries have now found their way into the body of this book, but here are some of the ones that got away.

I see pictures on the Net in all sorts of shapes, but mine are all in boxes how can I get a picture that's not box-shaped?
If the image that you want to put on your site is a GIF, this can be very easily achieved. Many graphics programs will allow you to export or save a GIF with a transparent background. All you do is nominate which colour you want to be transparent, and then export the file in what's called GIF89a format. When such a file is imported into your web page, it will appear without a visible background. You need to be just a little careful here, since this will involve making every instance of the stipulated colour transparent, not just those occasions when the colour forms part of the background. Generally, however, any difficulties this causes can be avoided by selecting a background colour which does not appear anywhere in the image, and using that as your transparent background colour.

JPEGs do not offer the opportunity to create transparent backgrounds, however. One option is obviously to convert your JPEG into a GIF: if this doesn't result in a satisfactory image, the easiest solution is simply to use a background colour in your graphics program which is identical to the background colour you use on your web site. So, if you create a picture of a guitar on a black background you may well still have a square graphic, but once you insert it into your web page which also has a black background all your visitors will be aware of is a guitar-shaped image. This trick can also work if you have a fairly muted tiled background to your site, but might involve you in a little bit of trial and error. Simply import a copy of the background image into your graphics program and create your image on top of that. The trial and error involved takes place when you insert the image into your web page: you have to ensure that your graphic fits in with the other 'tiles'. It's worth mentioning that this dodge will work well enough on most of your visitors' browsers, but for those browsers not configured to show backgrounds it's going to look rather messy.

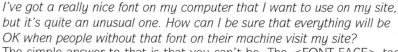

I've got a really nice font on my computer that I want to use on my site, but it's quite an unusual one. How can I be sure that everything will be OK when people without that font on their machine visit my site?

The simple answer to that is that you can't be. The <FONT FACE> tag will only work if the visitor has the specified font installed on his or her machine if it's not there the browser will work it's way through the options provided until it gets back to the default font.

Your only real recourse would be to save the text as a picture but this not a trick you can use too often as I've said earlier in this book it can be a useful way of dealing with headings, but it's important to remember that graphics files take much longer to load than plain text, so this is certainly not a way of dealing with body text.

How do I get a counter onto my site?

Figure 12.1 A counter adds a certain something to a site

Counters are dependent on something called a CGI (Common Gateway Interface) script. CGI scripts are small applications which actually run on the server on which your site is hosted, and it would be rare to find much CGI support coming with any basic ISP package. The exception to this rule is often the counter, and in many cases you'll find that your ISP provides this facility free of charge. The first step is simply to check with yours and, if they provide a counter CGI, follow their instructions for how you should use it.

If they don't provide this option then all is not lost, however, since there are a number of companies on the Internet who will let you use the CGI scripting on their server usually in exchange for a small ad of some sort. If this appeals to you then you could try www.digits.com/ or www.pagecount.com/; a quick search on the web should turn up a number of such companies for you.

This is inevitably a second-best option, and is likely to slow your page down a little, but it will certainly work – at least while the server holding the CGI script is up and running. This server actually registers the hit when someone visits your site, and the HTML on your page picks up a graphics file which represents some form of counter which is displayed on your page.

When I look at the source code for some sites I visit I sometimes see text between tags like this <!—TEXT —> what does it mean.

These are comment tags and are not HTML in themselves, but rather comments by the programmer about the HTML. These generally act as a jog to the memory for anyone going back to the coding at a later date, but are also pretty useful to anyone else visiting the site and trying to understand how it works.

How can I have a wallpaper background that changes as it goes across the page?

This effect is often used to replicate the spiral binding of an exercise book or a fade from one background colour to another. You need to use the same code as for any background (<BODY BACKGROUND="filename.GIF">), but make sure that the image you're calling up is very wide. If your 'tile' is wider than the viewer's browser window, then a new tile will be started at the left-hand margin all the way down the page, giving the effect that you're looking for. How wide is wide? It's all down to the typical size and resolution of the monitor that your visitor is likely to be using; though something like 600 pixels will work for a lot of people, for others it will result in a pretty confused browser page.

To really be on the safe side you might want to be thinking in terms of something like 1,200 pixels, since more and more people are moving away from the old standard 15-inch monitor and are working at higher resolutions. Be careful here, though, since the wider an image is the larger the file will be, and the longer it will take to download, so make it as short as it possibly can be if you can get away with a tile that's just five pixels high, so much the better.

Look, I really want to use that flashing text effect you talked about and wouldn't give the code for. I don't care how naff you think it is, I want it!
OK, I've already alluded to it a few pages back. Any text placed between a pair of <BLINK> tags wil flash on and off and on and off and on ... don't say I didn't warn you!

There are so many ISPs around today offering free access to the web and providing free web space do you think they're safe?
They're safe all right, in that they're not going to make your computer explode, but you might find that they don't always give quite so much support as other ISPs or that they expect you to carry free ads on your page in exchange for the web space. They're always worth a try, however, and if you register a domain name and then route visitors to your free site from that, you can always change that routing if you find them unsatisfactory and need to try another ISP.

How can I get a copyright sign onto my site?
Very easily. There is a whole range of what are called 'character entity codes' which will allow you to use fractions, accented letters, currency symbols and the copyright sign. Just key in &#169 as part of your HTML Mind you, I'm not sure just how much protection the copyright symbol would be on the Internet!

What are banners? Are they worth having?
They're essentially advertising hoardings you put on your site which will provide a link to someone else's. Personally I don't like them – they're graphic files, and so inevitably slow down the rate at which the page loads, and if I want to put a link to another site I'd as soon simply run a link from text. If your site gets really popular, however, you might be able to sell advertising space on your site, and put their banners up at a price. It certainly happens, but not to me!

SPECIAL CHARACTERS

&#169 gives ©
&#174 gives ®
&#64 gives @
&#36 gives $
&#163 gives £

14

Web resources and software

As this book went to press I checked all the URLs to make sure that they were still working. Inevitably some were and some weren't. Though I updated everything at that point it's inevitable that as time goes by some of these links will start generaing error messages. Your best bet, as always, is going to be to use the Internet to find what you want. I've already given you the URLs a number of shareware sites but if none of those can help you simply typing "shareware" into any search engine is going to get you everything you're looking for – and more! For the time being though, here are some links that you might find useful.

Backgrounds
If you don't fancy creating your own background tiles or other web graphics, there are thousands of sites where you can download ready-made ones. Here are just three:

www.best.com/~drzeus/Art/Textures/Textures.html
www.netscape.com/assist/net_sites/bg/backgrounds.html
http://netcreations.com/patternland/

Graphics programs
Graphic Convertor for Mac at http://www.lemkesoft.com
Graphic Workshop for PC at http://www.mindworkshop.com/alchemy/alchemy.html
Paint Shop Pro 4 for PC at http://www.jasc.com
GIFConverter for Mac at http://www.kamit.com/gifconverter/

GIF Animation programs
GIFBuilder for Mac at http://homepage.mac.com/piguet/gif.html
GIF Construction set for PC at http://www.mindworkshop.com/alchemy/alchemy.html

Sound programs
Cool Edit for PC at http://syntrillium.com
Goldwave for PC at http://goldwave.com
Soundhack for Mac at http://hitsquad.com/smm/programs/SoundHack
Sound Studio for Mac at http://www.felttip.com/products/soundstudio

Authoring programs
The time may well come when you decide that you do with some help

from an authoring program. There are a number of shareware and commercial programs, many of which are available on a 30 day free trial basis. You may find that these programs take rather longer to download from the internet than you want to put up with, and in that case your best bet is to have a look at one of the CDs that seem to be attached to just about every computer magazine. If you do want to try a download, however, then you might like to check out Dreamweaver (PC and Mac) Dreamweaver is at:

> http://www.macromedia.com/software/dreamweaver/

Homesite (PC) is at:

> http://www.allaire.com/Products/HomeSite/

The Internet abounds with shareware editors, all of which have their supporters. You can find very many of them at:

> http://www.window98.com/webedit.htm

while a couple more are to be found at:
Active Editor (PC)

> http://www.zdnet.com/downloads/stories/info/0,,001615,.html

Dutch's HTML Editor Pro V3 (PC)

> http://www.zdnet.com/downloads/stories/info/0,,000XER,.html

Finally, a free HTML editor worth tracking down is HTML Builder – you can find it at:

> http://www.flfsoft.com/index.html

Index

More music technology books from PC Publishing

Quick Guide to Analogue Synthesis

Ian Waugh
64 pp • ISBN 1870775 70 8
£6.95

If you want to take your synthesiser – of the hardware or software variety – past the presets, and program your own sounds and effects, this practical and well-illustrated book tells you what you need to know.

Quick Guide to Digital Audio Recording

Ian Waugh

64 pp • ISBN 1870775 68 6
£6.95

All modern music recordings use digital audio technology. Now everyone with a computer can produce CD-quality recordings and this book shows you how. It explains what digital audio recording is, how to use it, the equipment you need, what sort of software is available, and how to achieve professional results.

Quick Guide to Dance Music

Ian Waugh

64 pp • ISBN 1870775 69 4
£6.95

Dance – it's the music of the new Millennium. If you want to create Dance music, this highly practical book explains everything from how to create your own drum and bass lines to putting your music on the Web.

Quick Guide to MP3 and Digital Music

Ian Waugh

64 pp • ISBN 1870775 67 8
£6.95

MP3 files, the latest digital music format. What are they? Where do you get them? How do you use them? Will they make music easier to buy? And cheaper? Is this the future of music? All these questions and more are answered in this concise and practical book which explains everything you need to know about MP3s in a simple and easy-to-understand manner.

Check our website!
www.pc-publishing.co.

PC Publishing
Export House
130 Vale Road
Tonbridge
Kent TN9 1SP
UK

tel + 44 (0) 1732 770893
fax + 44 (0) 1732 770268
email
info@pc-publishing.co.uk
Web
http://www.pc-publishing.co.uk